Combating Internet-Enabled Terrorism:

Emerging Research and Opportunities

Emily Stacey
Swansea University, UK

A volume in the Advances in Digital Crime, Forensics, and Cyber Terrorism (ADCFCT) Book Series

IGI GLOBAL
DISSEMINATOR OF KNOWLEDGE
www.igi-global.com

Published in the United States of America by
IGI Global
Information Science Reference (an imprint of IGI Global)
701 E. Chocolate Avenue
Hershey PA 17033
Tel: 717-533-8845
Fax: 717-533-8661
E-mail: cust@igi-global.com
Web site: http://www.igi-global.com

Library of Congress Cataloging-in-Publication Data

Names: Stacey, Emily, 1984- author.
Title: Combating internet-enabled terrorism : emerging research and opportunities / by Emily Stacey.
Description: Hershey, PA : Information Science Reference, [2017]
Identifiers: LCCN 2016056031| ISBN 9781522521907 (hardcover) | ISBN 9781522521914 (ebook)
Subjects: LCSH: Cyberterrorism--Prevention. | Computer crimes--Prevention.
Classification: LCC HV6773.15.C97 S73 2017 | DDC 363.325/16--dc23 LC record available at https://lccn.loc.gov/2016056031

This book is published in the IGI Global book series Advances in Digital Crime, Forensics, and Cyber Terrorism (ADCFCT) (ISSN: 2327-0381; eISSN: 2327-0373)

British Cataloguing in Publication Data
A Cataloguing in Publication record for this book is available from the British Library.

Advances in Digital Crime, Forensics, and Cyber Terrorism (ADCFCT) Book Series

ISSN:2327-0381
EISSN:2327-0373

Editor-in-Chief: Bryan Christiansen, PryMarke, LLC, USA

Mission

The digital revolution has allowed for greater global connectivity and has improved the way we share and present information. With this new ease of communication and access also come many new challenges and threats as cyber crime and digital perpetrators are constantly developing new ways to attack systems and gain access to private information.

The **Advances in Digital Crime, Forensics, and Cyber Terrorism (ADCFCT) Book Series** seeks to publish the latest research in diverse fields pertaining to crime, warfare, terrorism and forensics in the digital sphere. By advancing research available in these fields, the **ADCFCT** aims to present researchers, academicians, and students with the most current available knowledge and assist security and law enforcement professionals with a better understanding of the current tools, applications, and methodologies being implemented and discussed in the field.

Coverage

- Cryptography
- Digital Surveillance
- Identity Theft
- Vulnerability
- Mobile Device Forensics
- Network Forensics
- Criminology
- Information Warfare
- Malware
- Global Threat Intelligence

IGI Global is currently accepting manuscripts for publication within this series. To submit a proposal for a volume in this series, please contact our Acquisition Editors at Acquisitions@igi-global.com or visit: http://www.igi-global.com/publish/.

The Advances in Digital Crime, Forensics, and Cyber Terrorism (ADCFCT) Book Series (ISSN 2327-0381) is published by IGI Global, 701 E. Chocolate Avenue, Hershey, PA 17033-1240, USA, www.igi-global.com. This series is composed of titles available for purchase individually; each title is edited to be contextually exclusive from any other title within the series. For pricing and ordering information please visit http://www.igi-global.com/book-series/advances-digital-crime-forensics-cyber/73676. Postmaster: Send all address changes to above address.

Titles in this Series

For a list of additional titles in this series, please visit:
http://www.igi-global.com/book-series/advances-digital-crime-forensics-cyber/73676

Combating Security Breaches and Criminal Activity in the Digital Sphere
S. Geetha (VIT University, Chennai, India) and Asnath Victy Phamila (VIT University, Chennai, India)
Information Science Reference • ©2016 • 309pp • H/C (ISBN: 9781522501930) • US $205.00

National Security and Counterintelligence in the Era of Cyber Espionage
Eugenie de Silva (University of Leicester, UK & Virginia Research Institute, USA)
Information Science Reference • ©2016 • 308pp • H/C (ISBN: 9781466696617) • US $200.00

Handbook of Research on Civil Society and National Security in the Era of Cyber...
Metodi Hadji-Janev (Military Academy "General Mihailo Apostolski", Macedonia) and Mitko Bogdanoski (Military Academy "General Mihailo Apostolski", Macedonia)
Information Science Reference • ©2016 • 548pp • H/C (ISBN: 9781466687936) • US $335.00

Cybersecurity Policies and Strategies for Cyberwarfare Prevention
Jean-Loup Richet (University of Nantes, France)
Information Science Reference • ©2015 • 472pp • H/C (ISBN: 9781466684560) • US $245.00

New Threats and Countermeasures in Digital Crime and Cyber Terrorism
Maurice Dawson (University of Missouri–St. Louis, USA) and Marwan Omar (Nawroz University, Iraq)
Information Science Reference • ©2015 • 368pp • H/C (ISBN: 9781466683457) • US $200.00

Handbook of Research on Digital Crime, Cyberspace Security, and Information...
Maria Manuela Cruz-Cunha (Polytechnic Institute of Cavado and Ave, Portugal) and Irene Maria Portela (Polytechnic Institute of Cávado and Ave, Portugal)
Information Science Reference • ©2015 • 602pp • H/C (ISBN: 9781466663244) • US $385.00

The Psychology of Cyber Crime Concepts and Principles
Gráinne Kirwan (Dun Laoghaire Institute of Art, Design and Technology, Ireland) and Andrew Power (Dun Laoghaire Institute of Art, Design and Technology, Ireland)
Information Science Reference • ©2012 • 372pp • H/C (ISBN: 9781613503508) • US $195.00

For an enitre list of titles in this series, please visit:
http://www.igi-global.com/book-series/advances-digital-crime-forensics-cyber/73676

IGI GLOBAL
DISSEMINATOR OF KNOWLEDGE
www.igi-global.com

701 East Chocolate Avenue, Hershey, PA 17033, USA
Tel: 717-533-8845 x100 • Fax: 717-533-8661
E-Mail: cust@igi-global.com • www.igi-global.com

Table of Contents

Preface

The table of contents for this work was completed one day before the brutal mass shootings in Orlando, Florida at a popular club for the Lesbian, Gay, Bisexual, Transgender, and Queer and/or Questioning (LGBTQ) community. The shooter pledged allegiance to the Islamic State (IS) in a phone call to the local authorities as well as on his Facebook page, before travelling two hours away from his home to perpetrate the attack. While the motivations in this case are numerous, political theorists would be remiss in not mentioning the very real threat of internet-enabled terrorism and the propaganda that has been widely circulated, inspiring numerous lone wolf style attacks.

The Islamic State formally distinguished itself from Al Qaeda in June 2014 and immediately began their quest to establish the caliphate by seizing Mosul; the third largest city in Iraq fell into IS control on June 20, 2014. This event marked the beginning of the legitimization of the group in the eyes of the international community. This legitimization was in no small way aided by the group's skilled use of social media in its initial phases of their invasion of Mosul to confuse the Iraqi military regarding the number of fighters. Brooking and Singer highlight this fact, stating "Media reports from region were saturated with news of the latest ISIS victory or atrocity, helping to fuel a sense of the Islamic State's momentum. There was no time to distinguish false stories from real ones" (2016). Undoubtedly, social media and the echo chamber it tends to produce, along with crafty co-opting of Western interest hashtags all assisted the Islamic State in seeming much more like a well-coordinated militia as it was moving into Mosul, than the "mere 1,500 fighters equipped with small arms" that they were in actuality (Brooking & Singer, 2016).

The U.S. and other Western governments missed a critical moment to strike in the initial phases of development for the Islamic State infrastructure in 2014. Mainly by discounting the severity of the situation, President Obama referring to the group as the terrorist "JV (junior varsity) team" (Contorno, 2014) only added to the confusion that the group was a much less serious threat than in reality. After the recording of American journalist James Foley's beheading was released on August 20, 2014, the pressure on Western governments, and most obviously, on the U.S. to respond intensified.

Since their establishment and declaration of jihad, IS has inspired, coordinated, and/or perpetrated a multitude of attacks around the world that have left thousands dead. Beginning in September 2014, with a lone wolf sympathizer being shot after stabbing two counterterrorism officers in Melbourne, Australia, a wave of IS (either affiliated or inspired) violence has spread around the globe and more influentially, through digital networks. The next attack on Western targets occurred in Canada less than a month later, when a 25 year-old who was self-radicalized assaulted two soldiers near Montreal with his car, killing one (Yourish et al., 2016). While these instances were individual actors, the Islamic State began increasing coordination and reach of its attacks as early as January 2015, when the group's Libyan affiliate held 23 Egyptian Christians captive, later releasing a tape of their beheading on the shores of the nation. While IS has conducted more methodical attacks in the tradition of its predecessor, Al Qaeda, it is more able to do so in the Middle East and regions that have a pre-established organization of fighters ready and willing to follow orders. Yourish et al. (2016) compiled a comprehensive list of Islamic State attacks to July 2016, and only Western attacks occurring in 2015 and 2016 have been perpetrated by numerous IS members, attacks in Western countries leading to 2015 have been individual actions rather than well-planned endeavors.

The internet has become a pervasive and invasive part of our existence, and extends from the private life into the public realm. Events such as Orlando, the attacks in Ottawa and Melbourne, as well as Paris and Brussels provide this work with its timeliness. In the digital age where technology, the internet, and social networking platforms are providing knowledge, communication, socialization, propaganda, and inspiration for global jihadists and extremists from all walks of life. Although in premeditated cases such as Paris and Brussels that were designed to harm or kill a large number of people in a coordinated attack, which was IS-supported and sponsored, the majority of Western attacks thus far have been lone wolf, meaning it is an individual or small number of individuals who are planning and conducting the attack. While they may pledge allegiance to radical Islamic groups, these attacks are not funded by the terror organization, simply inspired by their rhetoric and propaganda that is disseminated increasingly through various digital media outlets.

The importance of focusing research on the opportunities available to terrorist organizations in the digital age can translate into life-saving information, if plans can be interpreted in enough time with an effective intelligence community. The internet has long played a role in communication of ideology, which often leads to mobilization in the public sphere, whether for democratic goals, or as the world has witnessed with the adept and youthful attempts to inflict affective response on vulnerable populations through IS feeds, websites, and digital propaganda, encouraging a united front of global Muslims in their fight for a caliphate. The term caliphate invokes religious obligations for devout Muslims, and for the Islamic State's use the obligation of global Muslims to join the fight for the state in Iraq and Syria.

The role of the internet in global jihad has been marginalized by techno-utopians who have emphasized the democratic potential of digital technologies accompanied by the internet, including this author. However, the War on Terror that the West (led by the United States) has waged over the course of a decade has spilled over into the latest iteration of terror, the Islamic State. This group of radicalized, predominately young Muslims has infiltrated our public spaces online and challenged the West by recruiting many disenfranchised citizens through their skillful use of the places that these people communicatively dwell: online forums, social media platforms, and use of violent messages that are ensured to make mainstream media as well.

The existential threat of IS is not simply a mass-coordinated invasion of the Western world in a physical sense, but the digital psychological 'lone wolf' effect of internet recruitment and propagandizing that allows for the conversion of angry citizens around the world into IS operatives, working with or in allegiance to the group and its principles. The ability for the Islamic State to promulgate its content and show strength even in times of military defeat only helps to diminish attempts by governments around the world to show the reality of the caliphate. IS has empowered disaffected global citizens to, at the very least consume the organization's content, and at the most, proactively involve themselves in the jihad. As Torok (2013) notes, "ISIS's deliberately crafted public relations campaign has made social media sites—especially Facebook—a minefield for young, marginalized Western Muslims, some of whom may be vulnerable to indoctrination through exposure to the graphic imagery of ISIS's "pure" Islam." The potential for recruitment in digital spaces, particularly multi-modal communication platforms like Twitter has put Western countries at risk. Not only the risk of increased lone wolf activities but also for the build-up of hibernating armies, who will be ready to advance the Islamic State's cause once the "diaspora" that Federal Bureau of Investigations Director James Comey warned about in October 2016.

While concluding the text, the U.S., Iraqi, Kurdish, and Turkish military forces are building up for what could be the most important battle against the Islamic State, the retaking of Mosul in Iraq. This mission could be complicated, however, by the political tensions among the coalition forces fighting there. Most notably, the violent tension that has reignited between the Kurds and Turks, an ethnic and regional conflict that has raged for decades. Yet the U.S. has relied on the Kurdish peshmerga fighters as the boots on the ground in the fight against IS in Iraq and Syria, at one point controversially equipping the Kurds with more weapons and medical supplies in 2015 despite the Turkish government's protest.

As of October 12, 2016, Turkish troops are based at Bashiqa camp training "Sunni Muslim and Kurdish peshmerga units that Turkey wants to take part in the expected battle for Mosul" (Karadeniz & Gurses, 2016). However, Turkey taking a lead role in the battle has made Iraq feel as if its role has been diminished the role of its Shiite-led government. This conflict, which the U.S. has encouraged be resolved by the two nations without interference from outside governments, could impede the unity of the force and jeopardize the effective takeover of Mosul, the self-proclaimed headquarters of the Islamic State in Iraq (Karadeniz & Gurses, 2016). As the occupation of the Islamic State in Iraq and Syria comes to an end, it becomes necessary for governments around the world to ponder what comes next – a question that was left unanswered after the occupation and eventual removal of troops from Iraq. One strategy being explored by Syrian rebel group Jaysh al-Tahrir, who have established an internment camp for IS defectors as well as captured fighters in a village in Northern Syria (Sommerville, 2016). According to *BBC News*, 300 defectors and fighters (including Europeans) are being held at this internment camp for what its commander refers to as rehabilitation of the mind (Sommerville, 2016). The 'what next' question is crucial for both governments fighting extremism and extremists themselves. This question is greatly aided on the side of IS extremists by the ability for the group to effectively disseminate their ideology far beyond the territories that the group physically control through the adept use of the internet and social media.

This book explores the opportunities afford to internet-enabled terrorism via digital technologies and their evolution, the response of the State to cyber threats and combating the IS problem, and the role of non-state actors such as Anonymous in the fight to stop the influx of extremist rhetoric into mainstream digital culture. The goal is to provide thoughtful analysis of the Islamic State's use of technological advances and the State's response to date, and provide alternative recommendations that may allow for more effective identification and containment of jihadist dialogue in online spaces. The work poses questions for political and social scientists working in an interdisciplinary manner within digital media studies as well as provides suggestions to governments, the civil society, and individual citizens who are looking to disrupt the flow of jihadist, racist, or extreme nationalist propaganda via the internet. While this work does focus on terrorist organizations' use of digital tools to recruit and disseminate ideology, the world has witnessed over 2016, starting largely with BREXIT (but one could argue it began coalescing in the early months of the Donald Trump campaign in 2015) – a shift in international politics that has been facilitated by the rise of nationalist groups, fringe political parties, and aided by the phenomenon of 'fake news' through social media platforms. These topics will be of great interest to social scientists in the coming years as we attempt to understand the complicated new world order.

The book is structured in the following manner. Chapter one details the rise of internet culture among terror organizations beginning with Al Qaeda as well as the use of available technologies to communicate extremist ideologies and tactics to adherents around the world using the traditional media model that pre-dated the internet. The second chapter focuses on the rise of the Islamic State as a formal entity from an organizational split from Al Qaeda that began in the early 2000s, but did not officially manifest until 2014. This chapter also unveils the technological advantages afforded to the Islamic State due to its younger demographics and unique ability to market content directly at the most vulnerable audience, the youth. Chapter three considers the role of the state in countering extremist material and dialogue online, looking at models from the United States and United Kingdom as examples. The fourth chapter examines the role of non-governmental actors in combatting extremism online, including that of the hacktivist community, religious organizations (most importantly, Islamic groups) as well as civil society entities that may not associated with government.

The final chapter makes recommendations to the international counterterrorism community as well as the global civil society as to alternatives or suggested amendments to current programs to battle extremism that may be more effective in engaging the moderate Muslim community around the world to fight against the perversion of their faith. While the suggestions made are certainly not the only good ones out there, they provide a stepping-stone for Western governments to be inclusive in counterterrorism measures and providing for good faith with citizens around the world.

REFERENCES

Brooking, E., & Singer, P. W. (2016, Nov.). War goes Viral. *The Atlantic.* Retrieved from http://www.theatlantic.com/magazine/archive/2016/11/war-goes-viral/501125/

Contorno, S. (2014). What Obama said about Islamic State as a JV team. *Politifact.* Retrieved from http://www.politifact.com/truth-o-meter/statements/2014/sep/07/barack-obama/what-obama-said-about-islamic-state-jv-team/

Karadeniz, T., & Gurses, E. (2016, Oct. 13). Turkey says its troops to stay in Iraq until Islamic State cleared from Mosul. *Reuters.* Retrieved from http://www.reuters.com/article/us-mideast-crisis-iraq-turkey-idUSKCN12C0KF

Sommerville, Q. (2016, Oct. 12). Rebels set up internment camp for IS defectors. *BBC News.* Retrieved from http://www.bbc.com/news/world-middle-east-37629679

Torok, R. (2013). Developing an explanatory model for the process of online radicalization and terrorism. Perth, Australia: Springer. Retrieved from http://www.security-informatics.com/content/2/1/6

Yourish, K., Watkins, D., Giratikanon, T., & Lee, J. C. (2016, July 16). How Many People Have Been Killed in ISIS Attacks Around the World. *The New York Times.* Retrieved from http://www.nytimes.com/interactive/2016/03/25/world/map-isis-attacks-around-the-world.html

Chapter 1
The Development of Internet-Enabled Terror

INTRODUCTION

Internet is a battlefield for jihad, a place for missionary work, a field of confronting the enemies of God. It is upon any individual to consider himself as a media-mujahid, dedicating himself, his wealth and his time for God (Prucha, 2011, Pg. 46).

Digital technologies are assisting in the coordination, communication and sustainability of contemporary movements, for better or for worse. Much of the existing literature focuses on the optimistic and democratic potential of digital technologies as well as the internet (Castells, 1996, 1999, 2012; Gerbaudo, 2012; Hussain & Howard, 2011). Yet the imminent threat of cyber war, infiltration of sensitive databases, disruption of the global financial markets, and the preparedness of governments around the world to respond

DOI: 10.4018/978-1-5225-2190-7.ch001

has become a major question in the 21st century. Richard Clarke, former National Coordinator for Security, Infrastructure, and Counterterrorism noted,

The U.S. military is no more capable of operating without the Internet than Amazon.com would be. Logistics, command and control, fleet positioning, everything down to targeting, all rely on software and other Internet-related technologies. And all of it is just as insecure as your home computer, because it is all based on the same flawed underlying technologies and uses the same insecure software and hardware (Clarke & Knake, 2010, Pg. 31).

Most pressing is the utilization of digital technologies, social media, and the internet to aid in the facilitation of regimes, organizations, and groups that threaten the lives of humans (in the short-term) and global democratic governance (in the long-term). While the idea of terrorist groups or extremists using the internet for their own (oft not mainstream) agendas is not new, as organizations such as Al Qaeda, Hamas, Hezbollah, and more recently, the Islamic State, it is highly salient as more ruthless and pervasive groups are using digital tools more effectively to mobilize participants as well as support for their cause. This book addresses the evolving complexity of social media and internet use in contemporary terrorist organizations and the responses of the State (formal) and non-state actors (informal), such as Anonymous.

The co-dependent relationship between terrorist organizations and the media has been evident for a long time, as terrorists have relied on the traditional media (print, radio, television) to distribute their messages of ideology and destruction. Terrorists in the broadcast age had to plan very elaborate and strategic attacks on large-scale targets in Western countries or on Western-affiliated targets (Lockerbie bombing, various embassy bombings) in order to receive enough media attention to garner global recognition (Nacos et al., 2007). Terrorism by definition seeks to foster fear through attacks or threat of attack in societies that force governments and officials to pass legislation or take emergency measures that alter the function of a free (often democratic) society. The earliest example of methodical terrorist manipulation of the traditional media occurred in 1972, during the Munich Olympic games, when members of the Palestinian Black September group attacked Israeli athletes. This by no coincidence was the first Olympic games to be televised live and the first to be the location of a terror attack (Cosgrove & Bhowmick, 2013). Throughout the following decades, and the development of satellite and cable television, terrorist attacks and violence became a staple of news coverage, following the stories live and continuing coverage building up to the 24/7 news cycle that still remains.

Yet it is still important to note that while terror groups found an unwitting partner with broadcast media who wanted to increase viewership, thus advertisers, thus their bottom line, these large media corporations were/are owned by private individuals and/or regulated by the State. Terrorists and revolutionaries alike had to rely on available technologies such as cassette tapes (as used in the 1979 Iranian Revolution), pre-recorded videotapes (a staple of Bin Laden, who had them delivered via couriers to major broadcasters like Al Jazeera), and pamphlets or informational documents that were distributed through traditional networks such as through mosque populations. The 24-hour news cycle fed global citizens appetite to be constantly knowledgeable about their world, pushing a steady stream of news that disproportionately focuses on war, violence, and crime that simultaneously provided terrorist groups, such as Al Qaeda with the opportunity to broadcast their message (Soriano, 2008).

THE EARLY YEARS: AL QAEDA BUILDS A COMMUNICATIONS NETWORK

As previously mentioned, terrorist groups like Al Qaeda had to coordinate and execute large-scale attacks on Western or Western-affiliated targets in order to ensure critical global media coverage to spread their message. A consequence of the audience-ratings broadcast schema that relied on audiovisuals meant that terror groups resulted to attacks such as September 11, 2001 in the United States (Soriano, 2008). The broadcast media, and by association or indoctrination, the consumer now chooses violence and conflict over less salacious news stories, which in turn allowed for broader consumption of the events of September 11th. The news story endured for weeks and continues to be an annually broadcasted event on NBC channels in its entirety. While some Americans will view this as a memorial, the blatant manipulation of feelings and unadulterated re-living of that horrific day for many, and a glorious day for radical Islamists serves as a reminder of how reliant the broadcast media is on visuals for influencing viewership.

The communication between Osama Bin Laden and the world through broadcasted pre-recorded video tapes delivered to Al Jazeera that were consumed by the remainder of the global media, highlights the tenuous relationship that once existed between the terrorist organization and broadcast media. Bin Laden and Al Qaeda's use of Al Jazeera was a turning point in political communication of jihad, using the station to gain notoriety in the post-September 11th world (The Guardian, 2003). As a consequence of the remaining Arabic television stations being highly regulated and monitored by their governments, most Muslim viewers trust Al Jazeera's reporting as a relatively non-biased network regardless of where they may live (Soriano, 2008). In the aftermath of the September 11th attacks, Al Jazeera estimated subscriptions via satellite increased 300 percent during the month that followed (Soriano, 2008). Al Qaeda was at the mercy of the traditional media to shape and report their message as the corporation saw fit, and were dependent upon the outlet broadcasting their message to a wider audience, making it more likely the content would be consumed in the West.

The development of more portable technologies (video cameras, cell phones, laptops) as well as the proliferation of the internet and wireless capabilities by the late 1990s-early 2000s presented a new communication environment for terror organizations, as it did for democratic and other social/political activists around the world. By 2006, terrorists were harnessing the internet and platforms such as YouTube to broadcast their messages and conquests, often horrific scenes of violence, unedited to the masses for consumption. The rise of smartphones has also aided in the swift mobilization of terror organizations and their ability to maintain a distributed yet sustainable presence online – smartphones allows consumers to access the internet and communication tools while mobile. These tools have been used to capture the execution of Saddam Hussein, which was supposed to be secret. The video was leaked on the internet and viewed by millions around the world, furthering the anti-American and anti-occupation sentiment by Muslims throughout the Middle East (Burke, 2016).

But it was not until the rise of the Islamic State under the leadership of al-Baghdadi (who was much younger than Bin Laden) that the embrace of digital technologies by a terror organization would prove to be an effective multi-faceted tool for global jihad. Contemporary movements, including terrorist or extremist groups, are and have been making effective use of the advances in technology as well as new communicative mediums to spread their ideology beyond regional support to international awareness and recruitment efforts. According to Weimann,

The internet has enabled terrorist organizations to research and coordinate attacks, to expand the reach of their propaganda to a global audience, to recruit adherents, to communicate with international supporters and ethnic Diasporas... (2014, Pg. 2).

The effect internationally has been gradual yet staggering in the amount of so-called 'lone wolf' attacks that are being waged on citizens in Western nations in the name of IS or Islamic extremism (Boston 2013, Ottawa 2014, Sydney 2014, Texas 2015, Amsterdam 2015). The response by Western governments has been beleaguered and noncommittal, satisfied waging a technologically-based military strategy complete with drones, while relying on the Kurdish military to provide the bulk of the ground fighting, while conducting cyber counterterrorism cloaked in secrecy.

While global jihad has been coordinated in the last decade around the use of the internet and social media platforms in a more direct manner, cyber-terrorism has been a point of research since the early 2000s. Defined as the use of digital tools (computers, software, viruses) to damage or dismantle infrastructure that are necessary to a functioning society, including transportation, energy, or government functions (Chu et al., 2009). The U.S. National Security for Homeland Security identifies targets for critical infrastructure protections, including telecommunications and National Information Infrastructure, water treatment, food industry, energy facilities, public health systems, finance and banking services, and so on. These are crucial pieces of any state system, not just the United States, that if a terrorist wanted to target to attack whether digital or physical, could impede the development and sustainability of a society. According to Denning (2004), the goal of cyberterrorism is to wreak as much havoc and violence in a public sphere (that garners international attention) while coordinating and communicating in the shadows via the internet. Chu et al. identify Iraq Net that was created to conduct DDoS attacks on internet-based infrastructures meant to "overwhelm" and eventually render the service dysfunctional (2009, Pg. 2378). Or the Stuxnet virus that has been linked to the intelligence infrastructures of both Israel and the U.S., which was used to infiltrate and destroy Iranian nuclear sites. According to Zetter (2014), "Rather than simply hijacking targeted computers or stealing information from them, it escaped the digital realm to wreak physical destruction on equipment the computers controlled."

These cyber attacks, while certainly a danger to modern governments, have given way to the more sophisticated application of the internet and digital technologies to spread global jihad – returning to a traditional mission of Al Qaeda inspired terror based on the scores of 'infidels' that could be killed with a single attack, but unlike the early-to-mid 2000s. In the contemporary digital age, terrorists are using social media platforms, audio and video sites, photo-sharing tools, and developing their own web-based applications to inspire widespread attacks, as opposed to coordinating massive targeted events (i.e.: September 11, 2001). The term *global jihad* appeared in the international lexicon prominently in the 1990s when Osama Bin Laden declared his intentions to spread extremist ideology, and that the West was the greatest enemy of the Muslim world (Rogan, 2006). Global jihad was the driving force behind training camps that were established across the Middle East, but most notably in Afghanistan and the ensuing War on Terror that would be launched by the United States in 2003. The internet has become an indispensible tool for global jihadists, both in the early 2000s and more so now that the global network of terrorists have become decentralized.

Although they were not aware of the potential for and of social networking sites as propaganda machines at the time, Arquilla and Ronfeldt (1993: Pg. 27) describe a

netwar is an information-related conflict, including methods such as public diplomacy measures, propaganda and psychological campaigns, interference with local media and efforts to promote an opposition movement through computer networks,

which has become the tactics of contemporary terrorist organizations. As Arquilla and Ronfeldt note further,

Cyberwar and netwar are modes of conflict that are largely about 'knowledge' – about who knows what, when, where, and why, and about how secure a society, military, or other actor is regarding its knowledge of itself and its adversaries (1996, Pg. 4).

THE RISE OF THE DIGITAL JIHAD

Modern terrorist groups have moved beyond the strategic and long-term planning of coordinated, massive attacks to the short-term game of inspiring local radicals and disaffected citizens (Muslim or not) in Western countries to commit violence in the name of the organization. This shift allows the symbolic leaders to remain relatively sheltered from foreign intelligence agencies and confuses the military and/or diplomatic response among international governments. Highly dispersed networks, such as the global jihadist networks that Al Qaeda and now the Islamic State utilize to recruit, spread ideology, and propagandize are "very hard to deal with....What these have in common is that they operate in small, dispersed units that can deploy nimbly – anywhere, anytime" (Ronfeldt & Arquilla, 2001, Pg. 1). This dispersed network of terror has become quite evident to the international community during Summer 2016, which has produced multiple attacks on Western and Muslim nations alike in the name of the Islamic State (whether directly supported by the group or inspired by), spanning from Malaysia to France to Florida (Yourish et al., 2016).

Weimann (2004) noted that terrorists were using the internet as a communication and propaganda tool more than they were interested in attacking the infrastructure of the West. He emphasizes the traditional media's reliance on the internet to mine for trending and breaking news stories as much as the terrorist organizations rely on the net for unadulterated exposure of their message and ideology. Terror organizations in the digital age have embraced and used new technologies to their advantage by creating groups within their structure that are devoted to strategic communications, including the creation of professional quality video and magazine content, which is distributed via personal websites as well as social media platforms to be consumed and redistributed widely.

For example, in 2004 the Al Qaeda in Iraq organization appointed Abu Maysara al-Iraqi as their official spokesman and warned their followers to be weary of other jihadists' postings (Rogan, 2006). During the early years of jihadist communication, forums and blogs were widely used to disseminate information, so it became crucial for terror organizations to have control over the content being produced and distributed to potential sympathizers. As the internet proliferated and developed into an interactive medium, rather than a convenient bulletin board for propaganda, terror organizations have evolved or rather, devolved into less centralized, less hierarchical structures that outsource the jihad without strong central leadership or direction. As Rogan (2006, Pg. 17) states,

Many radical Muslim scholars maintain their official websites. Whether they are scholars living in exile, far from the community they address and

comment on, or scholars living among their target groups, the internet is a crucial means to easily reach a wide audience and spread often controversial and illegal propaganda.

Prucha notes that before 2011, Al Qaeda used a "jihadist cloud", which allowed the group to maintain a strong presence within "its virtual spaces and niches on the internet", although they were experiencing major setbacks on the battlefield in Afghanistan (2011). Since 2011, however, the world has witnessed the rise and increasingly more adept use of technological mediums by terror organizations that have spread their networks across the globe known as the "media mujahedeen" (Livingstone, 2004, Pg. 75), and more contemporary attacks have been live-streamed, tweeted in real-time, or inspired from online jihadist content. The "media mujahedeen" are the supporters of jihadist organizations who distribute ideology and propaganda through online networks that operate "through a dispersed network of accounts which constantly reconfigures much like a swarm of bees or flock of birds constantly reorganizes in mid-flight" (Fisher, 2015, Pg. 4).

Ronfeldt and Arquilla (2000) describe the phenomenon of "swarming", which is characterized as a seemingly nonstructural, unorganized manner of attack from all affiliated networks. Swarms occur without a centralized authority or direction, and in the context of terrorist or terrorist-inspired swarms, they are feeding the individualized, self-radicalization of actors across the world through constant dissemination of ideology and calling for attacks (the Islamic State during Ramadan, for example) and the realization of that call in various global locations. While the traditional media fostered and maintained a hierarchical order of producers and consumers of the news, the digital age complete with the internet and social media platforms have transformed the landscape of communicating jihad around the world.

As Prucha argues, "Whether via 'retweets' on Twitter, posting comments on YouTube videos, or 'likes' on Facebook, by embracing the emergent behavior and 'social search' which sites such as Twitter and Facebook facilitate, anyone can connect with and disseminate propaganda context outside of the 'classical forums'" (2014, Pg. 134). This is true for democratic movements using social media for mobilization as much as it is a reality in the digital age that unsavory actors, such as terror organizations will glom onto the available technologies that can provide a convenient and effective link to the world of supporters locally, regionally, and globally.

Brooking and Singer argue, "Social media platforms reinforce "us versus them" narratives, expose vulnerable people to virulent ideologies, and inflame even long-dormant hatreds" (2016). The traditional networks of family, friends, mosque/church, community are all still readily available but consolidated among a wider network via the internet, making messages (whether normatively good or bad) able to reach a much wider audience across members' networks. Denning notes, "One way of viewing the internet is as a vast digital library. The web alone offers several billion pages of information, and much of the information is free" (2001, Pg. 243). This is important as IS can use platform searches to identify potential sympathizers and initiate conversations to draw them into the ideology, target donors, and speak to potential recruits, those who would leave their homelands to join the battle in Iraq and Syria.

The Islamic State strategy encourages "leaderless jihad" or the idea of lone wolf terrorism to some extent, in which the symbolic leader or organization call upon followers to engage in attacks individually on behalf of the ideology. The concept of leaderless jihad is partly based on theories promulgated by militant strategist, Abu Musab al-Suri in the 2000s (Burke, 2016). This idea marks a distinct separation from traditional terror groups that existed in the broadcast communication era, the nonhierarchical, non-organizational, rhizomatic jihad where supporters and actors can consume materials online and become inspired to conduct their own attacks without direction from the top. It also allows for an increase in lone wolf attacks, as they are occurring more frequently, and are harder to detect because perpetrators are largely citizens living within the targeted population.

To reiterate, this "leaderless jihad" or increase in lone wolf terrorism is more possible now in part because of the existence and adept use of mobile digital technologies and the internet, which enables a decentralized network of propaganda-sharing, ideology-packaging, and recruiting opportunities. While news of the attacks may be shorter-lived than the major targeted attacks of the early 2000s (2001 New York, 2005 London), because these lone wolf events are occurring more frequently, the terrorist organization taking claim for the attack (or that the perpetrator has declared allegiance to) is receiving sustained coverage, on a near daily basis as of July 2016. As Neumann (2012, Pg. 9) states, "Arguably, the use of the Internet to radicalize and recruit home-grown terrorists is the single-most important and dangerous innovation since the terrorist attacks of September 11, 2001." The sustainability and pervasiveness of current jihadist ideology via online platforms, particularly social networking sites, has aided in the recruitment of IS supporters, both those who physically join the fight in Iraq and Syria, and those who self-radicalize by consuming digital content, including video, photo, audio, and communicating directly with other supporters or influencers in the organization.

The Islamic State conducted a campaign to recruit lone wolves in the United States through social media, calling on individuals to begin a campaign against Westerners, whether civilian or military (Levs & Yan, 2014). In March 2015, IS published a kill list on the internet with the names, addresses and photographs of one hundred military members in the U.S., again encouraging self-radicalized lone wolves living in America to act on the suggestion of the organization. Clearly, the internet and use of social networking platforms which enable multidirectional communication and swifter dissemination of propaganda have aided the Islamic State in their quest to inspire lone wolf attacks, as witnessed around the world in 2016 (Yourish et al., 2016).

RADICALIZATION: FANGIRLS AND APPROPRIATION OF CULTURE

Precht (2008) notes a correlation between the increasing number of jihadist websites and an increase in radicalization,

A recent empirical study of 242 European jihadists from 2001-2006, on the effects on the internet on radicalization, found that there is a correlation between jihadi web sites and propaganda on the internet and rapid radicalization.

This is not surprising as the amount of content out for consumption increases, so too would the ability for a person to convince themselves based on what they have read, watched, heard, or posted that they must now be an active participant in the movement. The more interesting finding is the inclusion of more women in global jihad, particularly in the message of the Islamic State, who have been targeting young Muslim women living in the West through social media sites (Huey & Witmer, 2016).

Social media has played an important role in increasing the involvement of women in global jihad, by providing a relatively inexpensive space for communication and spreading of jihadist ideology. In other words, social media provides a space for radicalization where one may not have existed in the traditional network of these young women. Traditionally, Muslim women are discouraged or disallowed from engaging in forms of public protest or conflict. Yet contemporary global jihad has embraced the role of the Muslim woman as facilitators and propagandists, as Cunningham notes (2007, Pg. 121),

Women have been supporters and family members of global Islamist groups like Al Qaeda for many years, but they have also reportedly been used to train women, run women's organizations and groups, participate as girls in Islamist summer camps...Although these activities are nonviolent, they are also frequent pathways to militancy for male members of global Islamist groups.

Huey and Witmer explore the nature of "#fan girls" who are typically regarded as 'wannabe' female supporters of terror groups such as the Islamic State who act on the fringes of the organization, mainly by following and retweeting influencers within their networks and promulgating ideology (2016). The authors studied 105 social media (mainly Twitter) accounts over nine months, 20 of which met the criteria of 'fan girl', including publicly perceiving their involvement in a terrorist organization as 'cool' and portraying their suspension from Twitter as a badge of honor to be boasted about (Huey & Witmer, 2016, Pg. 4). Demographics of the 20 fan girl accounts analyzed were varied: the average age was under 25 years old; the women were from different nations with varyingly open societies, including Sweden, Indonesia, and the United States; and their ethnicities were also stratified some Kurdish, Iraqi, and self-described Caucasians. There is no clear insight into how or who is predominately affected by Islamic State messaging via social media sites.

The fan girls symbolize a greater ethos of the Islamic State and their media strategy, the building of an internet community that is akin to a family. Once these fan girls or supporters have been accepted into the group, they belong to a "deeply connected group of youth who find a sense of community and kinship online" (Amarasingam, 2015). The Islamic State and other contemporary terrorist organizations have preyed on the vulnerabilities of disaffected, marginalized citizens (mainly targeting Western Muslims) to provide them with fellowship and the promise of a land where they can be free to practice their faith without persecution. Social media allows the anonymous legions to support and disseminate Islamic State without having directly pledged allegiance to the organization. These followers are able to choose their level of involvement from retweeting or posting propaganda to self-radicalization and carrying out attacks in their home countries, including many in the West in recent years.

Social media platforms have played a crucial role in the facilitating of the spread of propaganda, convening conversations in forums, through direct communication with potential recruits, and allowing for the swift conversion of global citizens into actors for global jihad. Most of the Islamic State's content is quite professional looking and the videos (ranging from beheadings to show strength, to near tourist-style walk-throughs of towns the group had captured) all have a Hollywood-style production quality. Javier Lesaca, a visiting scholar at George Washington University's School of Media and Public Affairs studied 1,300 IS propaganda videos found that "20 percent of the videos were directly inspired by Western content," including videogame Grand Theft Auto and the Clinton Eastwood film "American Sniper" (Brooking & Singer, 2016). The Islamic State has uncovered something that marketing professionals have long understood: "Compelling imagery matters far more than any accompanying text in determining whether or not something goes viral" (Brooking & Singer, 2016).

The Islamic State also takes advantage of social media platforms for live-streaming attacks or executions, providing for localized content that is disseminated internationally for consumption. While IS has shown a sophisticated knowledge of social media and a penchant for marketing their exploits to supporters and recruits around the world, the corporate and government response has been slightly effective in shuttering some of the Islamic State's influence on popular Western sites, such as Twitter. But not before the group made great ideological gains, spreading its tentacles into Southeast Asia, the MENA region (including the Sinai Peninsula, Libya, and Tunisia), and influence into Central Africa with regional satellite groups of Al Qaeda declaring allegiance to IS. The following chapter will explore the rise of the Islamic State and other contemporary terror organizations such as al-Shabab and Boko Haram, and their use of the internet and social media platforms.

REFERENCES

Amarasingam, A. (2015, Dec. 30). What Twitter Really Means for Islamic State Supporters. *War on the Rocks.* Retrieved from http://warontherocks.com/2015/12/what-twitter-really-means-for-islamic-state-supporters/

Arquilla, J., & Ronfeldt, D. (1993). *Cyberwar is Coming!* RAND Corporation. Retrieved from http://www.rand.org/pubs/reprints/RP223.html

Arquilla, J., & Ronfeldt, D. (1996). *The Advent of Netwar.* RAND Corporation. Retrieved from http://www.rand.org/pubs/monograph_reports/MR789.html

Arquilla, J., & Ronfeldt, D. (2000). *Swarming and the Future of Conflict.* RAND Corporation. Retrieved from http://www.rand.org/pubs/documented_briefings/DB311.html

Arquilla, J., & Ronfeldt, D. (2001). *Networks and Netwars: The Future of Terror, Crime, and Militancy.* RAND Corporation. Retrieved from http://www.rand.org/pubs/monograph_reports/MR1382.html

Brooking, E., & Singer, P. W. (2016, Nov.). War goes Viral. *The Atlantic.* Retrieved from http://www.theatlantic.com/magazine/archive/2016/11/war-goes-viral/501125/

Burke, J. (2016, Feb. 25). How the changing media is changing terrorism. *The Guardian.* Retrieved from https://www.theguardian.com/world/2016/feb/25/how-changing-media-changing-terrorism

Chu, H. (2009). Next Generation of Terrorism: Ubiquitous Cyber Terrorism with the Accumulation of all Intangible Fears. *Journal of Universal Computer Science, 15*(12), 2373–2386.

Clarke, R., & Knake, R. (2010). *Cyber War: The Next Threat to National Security and What to Do About It.* New York: Harper Collins.

Cosgrove, B., & Bhowmick, N. (2013, Aug. 5). Terror at the Olympics: Munich, 1972. *Time.* Retrieved from http://time.com/24489/munich-massacre-1972-olympics-photos/

Cunningham, K. (2007). Countering Female Terrorism. *Studies in Conflict and Terrorism, 30*(2), 113–129. doi:10.1080/10576100601101067

Denning, D. (2001). Is Cyber Terror Next? New York: U.S. Social Science Research Council. Retrieved from http://www.ssrc.org/sept11/essays/denning.htm.2001

Denning, D. (2004). Cyberterrorism. In R. A. Spinello & H. V. Tavani (Eds.), *Readings in CyberEthics* (pp. 536–541). Jones and Bartlett.

Fisher, A. (2015). How Jihadist Networks Maintain a Persistent Online Presence. *Perspectives on Terrorism, 9*(3).

Huey, L., & Witmer, E. (2016). #IS_Fangirl: Exploring a New Role for Women in Terrorism. *Journal of Terrorism Research, 7*(1), 1–10. doi:10.15664/jtr.1211

Levs, J., & Yan, H. (2014, Sept. 22). Western allies reject ISIS leader's threats against their civilians. *CNN News*. Retrieved from http://www.cnn.com/2014/09/22/world/meast/isis-threatens-west/

Livingstone, S. (2004). The challenge of changing audiences or, what is the audience researcher to do in the age of the Internet? *European Journal of Communication, 19*(1), 75–86. doi:10.1177/0267323104040695

Nacos, B., Bloch-Elkon, Y., & Shapiro, R. (2007). Post-9/11 Terrorism Threats, News Coverage, and Public Perceptions in the United States. *International Journal of Conflict and Violence, 1*(2), 105–126.

Neumann, P. (2012). *Countering Online Radicalization in America*. Bipartisan Policy Center. Retrieved from http://bipartisanpolicy.org/wp-content/uploads/sites/default/files/BPC%20_Online%20Radicalization%20Report.pdf

Precht, T. (2008). Homegrown Terrorism and Islamist Radicalisation in Europe: From Conversion to Terrorism. An Assessment of the Factors Influencing Violent Islamist Extremism and Suggestions for Counter Radicalisation Measures. Copenhagen: Danish Ministry of Defence. Retrieved from http://www.justitsministeriet.dk/sites/default/files/media/Arbejdsomraader/Forskning/Forskningspuljen/2011/2007/Home_grown_terrorism_and_Islamist_radicalisation_in _Europe_-_an_assessment_of_influencing_factors__2_.pdf

Prucha, N. (2011). Online Territories of Terror – Utilizing the Internet for Jihadist Endeavors. *Orient (Paris)*, iv.

Prucha, N. (2014). Celebrities of the Afterlife: Death Cult, Stars, and Fandom of Jihadist Propaganda. In R. Lohlker & T. Abu Hamdeh (Eds.), *Jihadi Thought and Ideology, Jihadism and Terrorism* (Vol. 1, p. 135). Berlin: Logos.

Rogan, H. (2006). *JIHADISM ONLINE - A study of how al-Qaida and radical Islamist groups use the Internet for terrorist purposes*. Transnational Radical Islamism Project. Norwegian Defence Research Establishment. Retrieved from http://www.ffi.no/no/Rapporter/06-00915.pdf

Soriano, M. (2008). Terrorism and the Mass Media after Al Qaeda: A Change of Course? *Athena Intelligence Journal*, *3*(1), 1–20.

We left out nuclear targets, for now. (2003, March 3). *The Guardian*. Retrieved from https://www.theguardian.com/world/2003/mar/04/alqaida.terrorism

Weimann, G. (2004). *Cyberterrorism: How Real Is the Threat? Special Research Report*. Washington, DC: United States Institute of Peace.

Weimann, G. (2014). New Terrorism and New Media. Washington, DC: Commons Lab of the Woodrow Wilson International Center for Scholars. Retrieved from https://www.wilsoncenter.org/sites/default/files/STIP_140501_new_terrorism_F.pdf

Yourish, K., Watkins, D., Giratikanon, T., & Lee, J. C. (2016, July 16). How Many People Have Been Killed in ISIS Attacks Around the World. *The New York Times*. Retrieved from http://www.nytimes.com/interactive/2016/03/25/world/map-isis-attacks-around-the-world.html

Zetter, K. (2014, Nov. 3). An Unprecedented Look at Stuxnet, the World's First Digital Weapon. *Wired*. Retrieved from https://www.wired.com/2014/11/countdown-to-zero-day-stuxnet/

Chapter 2
Contemporary Terror on the Net

INTRODUCTION

The networked global society that has been enabled by the internet and accompanying digital technologies and social media platforms has created an affordable, geographically and temporally unbounded, and semi-anonymous space where the exchange of dialogue, ideas, and calls to action have become increasingly more frequent. This networked space provides for both egalitarian democratic efforts as witnessed in the Arab Spring (2009-2013) as well as Hong Kong (2014) and the Black Lives Matter movement in the United States (2013-present). Yet many theorists dating back to the late 1990s have pontificated on the availability of this unbounded network to *bad actors*, including hacktivists, international criminal cartels, as well as terrorist groups (Conway, 2006; Hinnen, 2004; Soriano, 2008; Teich, 2013), which will be the focus of this book.

DOI: 10.4018/978-1-5225-2190-7.ch002

While research on the use of the internet by terrorist organizations is available in abundance, the correlation of social media platforms, more advanced technology, the dark web, and their exploitation by much demographically younger and savvier terrorist networks has provided a new landscape for research into not only the organization of these groups in the contemporary digital age, but also their goals, intentions, and their affective persuasion online in order to accomplish their mission. This has been particularly true for the Islamic State (also known as the Islamic State of Iraq and Syria (ISIS), the Islamic State of Syria and the Levant (ISIL), and more globally, as Daesh). The foundation for the Islamic State were established in the period after the U.S.-led invasion of Iraq in 2003, the group was formed out of Al Qaeda in Iraq, and is an unprecedented organization that combines terrorism with military capabilities. IS began its true rise in 2011 after the United States removed troops from Iraq, the moment was heralded as a celebration of seemingly, the beginning of the end of the War on Terror and notably, the government of Iraq being stable enough for the U.S. to dislodge from the puppet government.

Prime Minister al-Maliki began a crusade against Sunnis, including in the government, military and law enforcement within the Iraqi society after the U.S. removed itself from the situation, inflaming centuries old religious and sectarian tension in the region (Frontline, 2014). Although Al Qaeda in Iraq was essentially decimated after the American invasion, the militants that remained (becoming the foundation of the Islamic State) were Baathists from Saddam Hussein's military, battle-hardened terrorists who managed to escape death at the hands of an international coalition in Iraq, and were able to form an organization through the opportunity of the Syrian civil war. The Islamic State used the violence and anti-Assad sentiment in Syria to their advantage, marketing their message to a rebel groups fighting the government, this enabled the meager group that crossed the border into the Syrian conflict to grow its numbers and influence into the formidable group that exists today. IS has obtained advanced weapons from the Iraqi and Syrian militaries, including tanks, artillery, and chemical weapons that it has seized in successful combat engagements (Kam, 2015). This arsenal now reportedly includes armed drones, which were confirmed to have been used in an attack in Northern Iraq in early October 2016 that killed two Kurdish peshmerga fighters and wounded two French Special Operations troops (Gibbons-Neff, 2016). The group is also in possession of chemical weapons, which prompted the U.S. to target chemical weapons plants in September 2016, blaming IS for using chlorine and mustard gas (Starr, 2016).

IS distinguished itself from Al Qaeda as early as 2007 by using violence against civilians (Vitale & Keagle, 2014). Yet the formal announcement of the formation of the Islamic State from Baghdadi would not come until 2014. The division among the groups was clear and generational. While Al Qaeda, led by al-Zawahiri born in 1951, prefers more methodical, slow-developing plans to engage with the community to gain trust and support for their government, and targets were entities or officials of the state; IS uses violence against all, including women and children in extremely violent, and often public (whether executions are preformed as theatre for locals in ancient ruins, or recorded for mass consumption online).

In terms of leadership, Islamic State leader, Abu-Bakr al-Baghdadi, born in 1971 proved a strong influence on the global jihadist community by using a combination of physical and spiritual (ideological) power on the ground and in the hearts and minds of many, much of this strategy relied on available technologies to broadcast the message.

Framing the message is crucial to the ability of terror groups to elicit support that turns into active membership. IS focuses much of its messaging on the plight of Muslims, particularly those living in the West with the enemy, and how that enemy tears apart the foundation of the Islamic culture, religion, and identity. This, IS claims, can only be counterbalanced by the establishment of a caliphate for all Muslims. The recruitment of foreign fighters was

part and parcel of its leader's vision to restore the Islamic caliphate, a vision directly threatening the future of local regimes and representing the magnet attracting the thousands of young people streaming to Syria and Iraq to enlist" in the jihad (Kam, 2015, Pg. 22).

The ideological is combined, as Zelin (2015) explains, with the daily reinforcement that the IS military is continuing to gain ground and make achievements that attempt to legitimize and stabilize the caliphate. Terrorist groups today still have not started utilizing social media to the extent that IS has in the last two years to spur recruitment and inspire attacks around the world (Vitale & Keagle, 2014, Pg. 6).

DIGITAL TERRORISM AND THE OTHER

Brian Jenkins identifies emerging trends in terrorism, although he does not provide correlations between the new trends and the availability of the internet, many of the trends he notes can be amplified via use of the internet. In the interest of this work three of Jenkins' six concepts will be examined: 1) terrorism has become bloodier; 2) terrorists can now wage global campaigns; and 3) some terrorists have moved beyond tactics to strategy. Terrorism research notes the increase of not only lone wolf attacks but also the rise of more violent "bloodier" attacks (Jenkins, 2006, Pg. 118).

Terrorists are using more sophisticated weaponry and communications technologies to coordinate their attacks; where in the 1980s fatalities were in the hundreds, by the 2000s fatalities had reached the thousands with large-scale, high impact, soft target attacks. The Islamic State through its effective use of political communication via the internet, notably direct communication with potential recruits has inspired an increased surge in lone wolf and small cell attacks, those not coordinated at a organizational level, but encouraged by online tactics, communication or calls to action. Research in lone wolf terrorism notes that lone wolf attackers are more prone to display "some form of psychopathology as well as degrees of social ineptitude" (Teich, 2013, Pg. 2). One prominent study into lone wolf terrorism indicated that a majority of individuals (six out of 14 studied) suffered from mental illnesses ranging from bipolar disorder to schizophrenia to depression (Jasparro, 2010). Yet Bakker and de Graaf (2011) note that researchers should not generalize about the mental states of lone wolf terrorists, terrorists' backgrounds are all different, and some are psychologically disturbed while others are mentally healthy.

The psychological and emotional aspects related to communicating ideology and the foment of enduring attitudes of political change are important to consider when looking at digital protest movements. Hegel's concept of the "constitutive Other" (1977) should factor into current analyses of global terrorism and the use of digital technologies to recruit or create awareness of their cause. This concept emphasizes the relation of one's essential nature to an outward manifestation, or a point-of-view of binary nature of the essential and superficial, where each is the inversion of each other.

Social networking sites allow for the manipulation of the Other and collective action networks, particularly those that are mobilizing for a sustained engagement of dissent (IS) are using this 'Otherness' against citizens to persuade them into joining their ranks. IS has proven quite adept at seeping into mainly younger Middle Eastern women that have grown up in the Western world and preying on their feeling of isolation within a society that does not always accept or understand who they are fundamentally. So the lure of an Islamic State that is solely for them, where everyone will understand their plight and struggles, and there is a built-in family unit based around religious beliefs appeals to many youth living in the West, who fear for their futures after September 11, 2001 and a global War on Terror being waged for decades.

This shared emotional state is crucial to contemporary social movements as well as global jihad that are relying at least partially on social networking sites and digital technologies to assist in the spread of ideology and tactics. Where once having a solid, singular leader of a movement to espouse ideology and calls for change were enough, in the digital age of protest, having an engaged large network of loose, weak ties is much more important than having a small, extremely active network of strong ties.

The ability for IS to recruit, coordinate and execute as well as inspire global attacks using digital technologies and an adept message of confusion, alienation and understanding to be found by joining their movement has aided the group in its nearly three-year development, and takeover of large swathes of Syria and Iraq. As Stern states (2003, Pg. 283),

Unless we understand the appeal of participating in extremist groups and the seduction of finding one's identity in oppositions to Other, we will not get far in our attempts to stop terrorism.

So the anger and hate that groups like the Islamic State are honing in on and cultivating among Western Muslims or disaffected citizens becomes effective in recruiting individuals actors, but also in sowing seeds of discontent and distrust of the Other in Western society, which keeps the cycle of hate, attacks and fear churning.

As previously stated, lone wolf attacks are on the rise in the West, Spaaij (2010) noted that the United States has experienced more lone wolf terrorism than the other fourteen countries studied (all Western). Teich (2013, Pg. 9) studied lone wolf terrorist attacks between 1990 and 2013, there were a total of 73 attacks: 27 lone wolf attacks and 46 attempted attacks by Islamic extremists, with 29 out of 73 attacks occurring within the span of three years, between 2010 and 2013. The United States was the nation targeted most often, accounting for 63 percent of all attacks (46 total attacks). When political scientists examine the factors that may contribute to this uptick in lone wolf attacks in the United States, it must be noted that it is much easier for self-radicalization online and to coordinate an attack in a place where you live, than to send hordes of fighters to attempt to infiltrate the U.S. and plot a large-scale attack.

In 2003, Stern recognized the growing threat of lone wolf terrorism and showed through research that there was a correlation between the increase of individual attacks and the proliferation of more powerful weapons. Although Stern is referencing a quote from Ayman al-Zawahiri's autobiography, in which he encourages the youth of Islam to arm themselves to defend their religion and themselves with pride, this sentiment is particularly chilling in the contemporary United States where self-radicalization and the availability of high capacity firearms makes a tumultuous combination. Stern notes, "As increasingly powerful weapons become more and more available, lone wolves, who face few political constraints, will become more of a threat, whatever their primary motivation" (2003, Pg. 34). Lone wolves, to reiterate, tend to mix ideological motivation with personal grievances as the world witnessed most recently with the Orlando night club shooting, the perpetrator swore allegiance to the Islamic State in the hours before the attack on the LGBTQ night club, which he had allegedly frequented, concealing a side of himself that directly conflicted with his religious inclinations and likely resulted in psychological issues regarding identity.

According to Koerner (2016),

...When Americans perpetrate violence in the name of the Islamic State, they tend not to be strict adherents of the organization's ideology, but rather disturbed individuals who hope to layer a political façade atop their personal grievances – grievances sometimes known only to themselves,

reiterating the description of lone wolves as often half-heartedly supporting the terror organization, while harboring personally felt injustices that manifest in the form of an attack.

Going back further to the 2009 mass shooting at Fort Hood, Texas perpetrated by Major Nidal Malik Hasan, who was working as an Army psychiatrist at the time of the attack that killed 13 people. Hasan had a life history of devout Sunni religious practice but was not radicalized until after the death of his parents, and subjection to deployment in the Iraq War, which Hasan resisted (Teich, 2013). Hasan was inspired by the teachings of Al-Awlaki, a radical American-born Yemenite preacher, which further enraged Hasan about the killing of Muslims in the War on Terror in both Iraq and Afghanistan. Although Hasan showed signs of self-radicalization stemming from a lifetime of devout religious practice that eventually coincided with the global War on Terror and his personal feelings regarding the ethics and politics of the engagement. The combination of religious devotion along with political obligations (military) manifested conflicting feelings for Hasan, there were no links to terrorist organizations found on Hasan's computers during the investigation and his court martial. Teich (2013, Pg. 5) emphasizes that "terrorists' organizational narratives assist in the externalizing of these individuals' [lone wolves] personal grievances as part of the Islamic radicalization process", so while lone wolves may act in accordance with shared tactics and ideologies of a well-known terrorist organization, their mission is often mixed with their own personal vendettas simultaneously.

The contemporary iteration of terrorism has become not only adept at utilizing the resources available to them via the internet, but also not to overreach in terms of strategy, coordination, and execution of attacks. Terrorist attacks have digressed in the number of fatalities, no longer in the thousands with a single attack, as the world witnessed during September 11, 2001. Yet the frequency of attacks by lone wolf inspired actors combines fatalities into the thousands. According to Jenkins (2006, Pg. 127),

Terrorist strategy is based not on achieving military superiority but rather on making the enemy's life unbearable by attacking incessantly; by inflicting endless casualties; by destroying tourism and discouraging investment, and thus inflicting economic pain; and by carrying out spectacular operations like 9/11; terrorism at its core is about the disturbance of the norm, causing such fear and anxiety that entire societies must adapt their behavior in order to have the perception of safety.

It is this author's opinion that more frequent lone wolf style attacks have outpaced large-scale events such as September 11th due to the amount of planning, coordination, and transference of resources overseas. It is much less risky for autonomous actors carrying out attacks in the name of, and in allegiance to the larger terrorist organization. For example, over the month of Ramadan 2016, in just one week from June 28-July 4, there were three major attacks: the first occurred June 28 at Istanbul's Ataturk airport that killed 36 and injured an additional 147 people (Tuysuz & Almasy, 2016); the next on July 1 was an attack on an international fine dining restaurant in Dhaka,

Bangladesh that killed 28 people, 20 of whom were hostages (Hammadi et al., 2016); and finally, detonation of a truck bomb in a predominately Shia neighborhood of Baghdad killed nearly 300 people on July 3. The Islamic State has claimed responsibility for two of the three aforementioned attacks, while not publicly noting their involvement in the Istanbul plot, the pattern of the attack closely resembles that of the Brussels airport and metro attack.

USE OF AVAILABLE MEDIA IN THE PROMOTION OF JIHAD

Arguably, the 21st century internet with its ever-increasing multimodal platforms, levels of encryption, and lack of regulation has made the internet a place of golden opportunity for groups like the Islamic State or Boko Haram. Not only to share their jihad through videos, audio, and photographs, but also to prey on disaffected Western Muslims living on the outside of their society and enabling them to take action within their own countries. Koerner notes,

Unlike Al Qaeda, which has generally been methodical about organizing and controlling its terror cells, the more opportunistic Islamic State is content to crowd source its social media activity – and its violence – out to individuals with whom it has no concrete ties (2016).

The necessity for fighters and supporters to cross borders to training in the Middle East has become obsolete. In the digital age, radicalization is as simple as clicking on the correct website, connecting to the right communications network, and conducting a Google search for the recommended content. This book will emphasize the growing number of lone wolf style attacks in the West and the ability of modern terrorist organizations to affect citizens living in nations outside the Middle East to the point of action. Unlike terrorist groups of the pre-internet (1980s) and development/proliferation period of the internet (1990s-2004), the groups that exist today are utilizing social media platforms to directly communicate ideology to potential followers, and inflict horror in (or upon) the West (as was the case in the most recent attacks outside a U.S. consulate building in Saudi Arabia as well as the fine dining restaurant in Bangladesh) without having to send en masse fighters to U.S. or European borders.

As former White House Cyber Security Chief Richard Clarke (2004) notes, "Terrorists use the internet just like everybody else", and the ways in which terrorist groups are using the internet has adapted to new platforms, capabilities, and available technologies as well as the adaptation of strategies for jihad. Conway (2006, Pg. 11) provides a categorization of terrorist uses of the internet, noting five standard applications of the net in promulgating the organization's mission, including: 1) information provision; 2) financing; 3) networking; 4) recruitment; and 5) information gathering. The five categories remain highly relevant in contemporary internet use by terrorist organizations. This work will focus on provision of information, or the spreading of ideology and propaganda, as well as networking, which this author argues encompasses recruitment through involved, personal and direct communications with potential members or actors, this was something the traditional media was unable to accomplish.

While early terrorist organizations had to rely on coordinating attacks so large as to attract the attention of television producers, print publishers and radio broadcasters, contemporary groups have a constant connection to their own websites, social media networks, and YouTube channels to broadcast their message in an unadulterated or edited fashion. The traditional media apparatus was able to define the terrorist groups and their intentions before the internet, and now global citizens are able to consume their message without the filter of decency or foreign policy explanations to decide for themselves if the cause is righteous. Conway notes that although the intended audience for consumption of terrorist propaganda might be small, a "well-designed and well-maintained website gives a group an aura of legitimacy" (2006, Pg. 12).

This is clearly amplified in 2016, where terrorist groups are not only expected to maintain a constant online presence but to keep the content fresh (i.e.: the Islamic State's monthly *Dabiq*). In a report released in October 2015 entitled *Documenting the Virtual Caliphate*, IS releases 38 new items per day, including extended videos, documentaries, audio, and instructional documents in numerous languages. In April 2016, an Islamic State published online magazine, *Dar Al-Islam*, put out an issue devoted to online safety and privacy, which gave explicit instruction on using various applications and platforms to access IS content safely (Frenkel, 2016). It is interesting to note that *Dar Al-Islam* is published in French, and writing in July 2016, France thus far has experienced the most deadly lone wolf attacks in the Western world at the hands of IS.

Most recently, on July 14, where a celebration was marred by a Tunisian-born French citizen who plowed a commercial refrigerated truck through a large crowd assembled in Nice to watch a fireworks display commemorating the French holiday of Bastille Day, leaving 84 people dead. This comes after the French government released a mobile application in June 2016 to alert and transmit information to citizens during a terrorist attack, known as the Systeme d'Alerte et d'Information aux populations, or the Population Alert and Information System (Newman, 2016). The app is able to track users' locations to send timely updates as to the dangers in their immediate environment, and enables users to set up alerts for eight different postal codes. While it is a step by the French government to provide security and information to their citizenry, the application begins sending alerts within 15 minutes of the government declaring there has been an attack or event, making social media a much more efficient, but not always accurate news source.

Al Qaeda and other contemporary terrorist organizations have moved their online presence to YouTube, Twitter, Facebook, Instagram, and other social media outlets. Abu Mohammed al-Golani, the head of an Al Qaeda branch that operates in Syria known as the al-Nusra Front, utilizes Facebook and various other social media sites frequently. In August 2013, al-Golani vowed

unrestrained rocket attacks on Alawite communities, alongside attacks on President Bashar Assad's government in revenge for an alleged chemical strike – a message that was posted on Facebook and Twitter, as well as on a militant website that often broadcasts the views of Al Qaeda and other extremist groups (Weimann, 2014, Pg. 2).

Networking emphasizes the ability in the digital age for terrorist (and other NGOs, social movements, etc.) to become less centralized and non-hierarchical. Networking allows for the dissemination and coordination of attacks that are independent of the small, symbolic leadership but still connected to the terrorist organization through inspiration, ideology, or allegiance pledged by the perpetrators. The internet has allowed for the dispersion of tactics, coordinated attacks, and ideology well beyond the nations or even the region that the terror groups occupy. Many theorists note the rise of *global jihad* where the ideology of extreme Islamists has permeated through the world in reaction to recent political events such as the War on Terror (Conway, 2006; Torok, 2013, etc.). So while there may be stated leaders in these terror organizations that handle certain aspects of the mission (such as fundraising, weapons coordination, public relations), "there is no specific heart or head that can be targeted" (Conway, 2006, Pg. 14).

The world is witnessing how true this statement is with the death of top members of IS being replaced overnight. Torok (2013, Pg. 9) notes, "Although key leaders may be influential, power is not possessed by an individual; it is a circular relation that flows through many networks and individuals that make up that network" - making the internet and social media platforms a great environment to coordinate global jihad. Although the largest attacks recently in Brussels and Paris have been communicated through older technologies such as burner or temporary cell phones, the adoption of Islamic State tactics and ideology has been a coordinated digital effort on behalf of their organization. This digital dissemination has increased the network of terrorists or radicalized individuals to global reach. As Arquilla, Ronfeldt, and Zanini (2000, Pg. 41) articulate,

Terrorists will continue to move from hierarchical toward information-age network designs. More effort will go into building arrays of transnationally internetted groups than into building stand alone groups.

Hierarchies are more vulnerable than the network model that emphasizes strength and coordination among levels rather than a top-down structure.

Jenkins (2006) notes that Al Qaeda was one of the first groups to model its organization on international business models, featuring "hierarchical but not pyramidal, loosely run, decentralized but linked [operations…that are] able to assemble and allocate resources and coordinate operations, but hard to depict organizationally or penetrate" (Pg. 123). This organizational structure was adopted by the fringe wing of Al Qaeda that became the Islamic State that boasts a strong presence of physical occupation in Syria and Iraq, but occupy the hearts and minds of disaffected Muslims globally via the internet, social networking, and deft propaganda marketing.

The use of a monthly magazine to keep would-be terrorists and supporters aware about the global fight, tactics that can be used to conduct their own personal jihad, and ideology to keep the legions motivated are published in the Islamic State's *Dabiq*. The magazine was first published in 2014 and continues to put out fresh content monthly via the dark web. Weimann (2014) notes the potential of the dark web to provide a relatively cloaked space for the dissemination of jihadist and terrorist propaganda. The dark web has been linked to numerous controversial developments in the digital age, including

WikiLeaks, Bitcon (the currency of the dark web), and criminal enterprise The Silk Road, which existed for two years. The lure of the dark web's decentralized and anonymous networks allow for criminals and terrorists alike to conduct business on a level that is difficult for government officials to control, monitor, or stop. The Islamic State increasingly has turned toward the dark web in the aftermath of the attacks on Paris in November 2015, after which the hacktivist organization Anonymous declared war on the group's digital communication apparatus. Hussain and Saltman (2014) conclude that while "Islamist forums and chat rooms in English and French are still widely available, a large portion of more extremist Islamic discourse now takes place within the dark web."

The Islamic State has responded tactically to increased government and non-government surveillance and disruption of mainstream communication channels, such as Twitter. They have instead migrated their socialization onto encrypted cell phone applications such as Telegram, which unveiled the ability to create channels, enabling the Islamic State to create their own known as *Nashir* (distributor in English), allowing for the free and wide distribution of jihadist ideologies. Pavel Durov, CEO of *Telegram* noted in an 2015 interview with the *Washington Post,* "Privacy, ultimately, and our right to privacy is more important than our fear of bad things happening, like terrorism" (Dewey, 2015). This sentiment is one that corporate officials are having to balance in the realm of free speech and national security.

However, the Islamic State harnessed the tools and tactics that Al Qaeda initiated, according to Jenkins (2006), the group used online monthly manuals to provide instruction to their followers around the world, led by shared ideology the periodical encouraged believers to wage their personal jihads autonomously of the central organization, or leadership. Stern (2003) articulates the terror world's shift from jihad on central governing organizations and entities of the State, to a more egalitarian style of attack on Western civilians beyond the coordinated attacks planned by the organizational structure. Stern (2003) notes that Osama Bin Laden's calls to jihad began in 1992 when he urged believers to kill American and Western soldiers stationed in Saudi Arabia; the second call came in 1996 via a 40-page manifesto that listed cruel acts committed on the Muslim world, predominately by Western nations (militaries); and the third, which was released in February 1998, called on his followers to target and attack Western civilians rather than the military-state complex.

Bin Laden still had to rely on the traditional media apparatus to promulgate his ideologies and calls for jihad. However, new communication technologies create interactive platforms through which individuals and communities share, co-create, discuss, and modify content (Weimann, 2014). Weimann also notes the increased time spent on social media sites in the United States as a veritable pool of recruits for terrorist organizations, with an increase from 88 billion minutes in July 2011 to 121 billion minutes in July 2012, an increase of 37 percent in a single year.

Wieviorka (2004, Pg. 43-45) was one of the first theorists to characterize the varying relationships that terrorist and the media may have, including complete indifference (this is uncommon), relative indifference (terrorists are not concerned with being on the news but are aware of the power that they provide), media-oriented strategies (many terror groups operate under this characterization, which note terrorists want to manipulate the media in order maximize coverage of an attack, event or promulgating ideology), and complete breakaway (this occurs when terrorists view the media as enemy combatants that must be destroyed along with other infidels. The world is witnessing a surge in the breakaway, as groups like the Islamic State are purposefully capturing Western journalists for public, or recorded executions.

Arguably, the traditional media including television and print outlets are still integral aspects to the contemporary landscape of global jihad. Yet the internet has altered the structural element of communication and organization, moving away from the hierarchy of the broadcast media, and allowing citizens and terrorists to dictate the news from the bottom-up and in a multidirectional fashion allowing for instant diffusion of ideology and calls for action. The infusion of the internet in Al Qaeda and other terrorist organizations' strategies allows for their message to be spread unperverted of the editorial framing of the mainstream outlets. This has become increasingly important as modern terror groups dislike the traditional media as their targeted audience (Soriano, 2008). Soriano notes, "From Al Qaeda's point of view, the news media are principally responsible for the liberating message of the Salafist Islam being ignored or distorted. This makes it impossible for the Jihad to penetrate in large sectors of the Muslim community, which finds itself immersed in the most pure ignorance and error" (2008, Pg. 7).

According to Soriano (2008, Pg. 7-11), jihadists perceive the media in various negative connotations including their role as a pacifier to the global Muslim population, keeping the population blind to the motivations of the

West; constructing a straw man of strength on behalf of Western governments in response to global jihad; and contributing to the use of violence against Muslims as a way to reinforce Western democratic principles over the forces of evil. This understanding about the role of the media in perception of the terrorist organization by global audiences has understandably led to an increased role for the internet in becoming the main vehicle of communication among and between global jihadists and the organizational structures in the Middle East. Soriano highlights,

Al Qaeda understands that the type of relationship that it has with the mass media in recent years highly threatens the organization's and its members' security. Its desire to eliminate these vulnerabilities has led the terrorist organization to put new technology to even more use (2008, Pg. 15).

It is crucial to note here that the new media (digital technologies and the internet) has not replaced traditional mechanisms of political communication of jihad, but has enhanced and supplemented those traditional networks. Because the traditional media use the internet to find trending stories in order to build a broadcast or the next day's paper, the online presence and public relations machine of terror organizations have become crucial in dissemination of ideology. This cyclical relationship between the traditional and digital media has made simply the existence of jihadi websites, content, forums, etc. more likely to receive some sort of mainstream attention, and if not, it is still spreading the message via the internet. The relationship has also blurred the responsibility of morality and decency in reporting the news. Television stations that were once reluctant to broadcast scenes from war or brutality have become less concerned when it comes to the consumption of terrorist content, most notably the IS beheading videos, making the mainstream media accomplices of terrorists by normalizing their behavior.

SOCIAL MEDIA, THE INTERNET, AND TERRORISM

Terrorists use the internet and social media as propaganda channels, radicalization avenues, and recruitment tools. Due to the amount of freely available information found on social media platforms such as Facebook, where the default is to show all published information besides one's birthday and contact information, terror organizations have a much easier time recognizing and accumulating lists of potential recruits or followers to assist in the cause. Weimann notes that social media outlets allow terrorists to use traditional media strategies such as narrowcasting, which aims messages at specific segments of the public "defined by values, preferences, demographic attributes, or subscription" (2014, Pg. 4). The nature of social media sites is that they allow for customization or individualization of the message, which makes the sites a great tool for recruiting younger membership into terrorist organizations. Anthony Bergin highlights this point, saying that terrorists perceive and use youth-heavy websites as recruitment tools "in the same way a pedophile might look at those sites to potentially groom would-be victims" (Bergin, 2008).

The proliferation of the internet and social media platforms among terrorist organizations culminated into a formal call for "electronic jihad" from Al Qaeda in May 2012 (CNN Wire, 2012). Internet platforms that are used to promote electronic jihad are also used in an organizational manner to provide tactics and training, collecting information about potential recruits and/or followers, and coordination. This includes the introduction of virtual training camps that teach would-be jihadists how to make bombs and weapons, hacking skills, and other instructional materials (Weimann, 2014). The perpetrators of the 2008 terrorist attack in Mumbai used digital technologies, including mobile GPS devices to plan and execute the attack, Google Earth satellite images, and cell phones to keep them up-to-date regarding hostages.

Facebook is a medium of choice among terror organizations, due to its high level of penetration in the Middle East, reaching 67 percent in 2010 (Weimann, 2014). Through Facebook, terrorists look for and target disaffected Westerners and marginalized Muslims. The U.S. Department of Homeland Security (2010) noted various uses of the internet by terror organizations, including: a gateway to extremist sites and radical online content by linking on Facebook group pages, and as a media outlet for terrorist propaganda and extremist ideological messaging. Twitter has more recently emerged as *the* platform of choice by terrorist organizations, becoming more popular than Facebook to disseminate propaganda as well as to communicate among leadership and the extended network. The Islamic State has effectively co-opted extremely popular and globally pervasive hashtags during large events, notably during the 2014 World Cup, the group flooded #Brazil2014 and #WC2014 with gruesome photos and horrifying messages of violence. One such message spread through World Cup trending hashtags was a video entitled *There is*

No Life without Jihad, which features British members of IS fighting on the battlefields. Weimann states that terrorists' use of Twitter takes

advantage of a recent trend in news coverage that often sacrifices validation and in-depth analysis for the sake of almost real-time coverage....under these conditions, mainstream media may take tweets as a legitimate news source (2014, Pg. 8).

Twitter has proven to be a stronghold for the Islamic State's decentralized communication strategy, and enables the group's influencers to gain the trust and support of potential recruits around the world using clever marketing and personal contact (i.e.: direct messaging). Islamic State fighters have also capitalized on the glossy Hollywood video production and understand the pervasiveness of gruesome photos as a marketing tool, but the group has more than any other terror organization grasped the necessity to make their jihad personal to recruits. The near intimacy that IS operatives use while luring disaffected global citizens into the web has been a cornerstone of their success in receiving an estimated 30,000 foreign fighters since 2014 (Brooking & Singer, 2016). The authors note a Dutch IS member fighting in the caliphate maintained an active Tumblr presence, with photos ranging from "his fellow fighters at rest; his newborn baby; even his cat, stretched alongside a suicide belt" (ibid., 2016).

It is important to again distinguish the Islamic State's use of social media as opposed to more traditional media to disseminate ideology and propaganda. Where terror organizations that are more insular and traditional rely on spreading messages through proper channels from the leadership to the masses, the Islamic State has advantageously co-opted the democratic character of the internet and social media to allow anyone and everyone (including those who oppose them) to join and promulgate the conversation. Terror organizations based in Africa such as The Mujahideen Youth Movement, Al Qaeda in the Lands of the Islamic Maghreb, the Oromo Liberation Front, the Movement for the Emancipation of the Niger Delta, as well as Boko Haram all maintain a Twitter presence and will provide content in English to target Western audiences. Although Twitter and various other social media platforms leave the potential for corrupting the message or feed by flooding it with memes such as IS Chan, an anime girl meant to shame IS members by depicting her in various real footage scenes, the benefit for recruitment obviously outweighs the negatives as IS has only increased its use of Twitter (Vitale & Keagle,

2014). As 2016 U.S. presidential candidate, Donald Trump says, "There is no such thing as bad publicity."

Contemporary terrorist organizations such as the militant group Al-Shabab use Twitter in increasingly advanced manners. During the 2013 rampage on Westgate Mall in Nairobi, Al-Shabab militants used Twitter to provide live commentary on the attack. Directly following the attack, a Somali-based Al Qaeda affiliate tweeted the rationale for the attack on the mall and provided operational details in real-time. The attack that killed 72 people was the first time a terrorist group claimed responsibility via Twitter (Weimann, 2014). Twitter has become an important tool for communication and coordination during movements and terrorist attacks alike, due to its real-time updates as well as photo, audio, and visual capabilities. This skillful adoption of not only the internet, but also social media platforms that allow for personal communication and consumption of extremist ideology has given global terrorist organizations an upper hand in waging electronic jihad. Weimann states,

Terrorist followers, sympathizers, converts, and newcomers find in the new media a much lower threshold to access terrorist-produced and terrorism-related content than they faced in discovering and signing up for access to the hardcore forums (2014, Pg. 20).

The average citizen is now aware when a new video message is posted or published from the Islamic State. Traditional media outlets are redistributing the content in neatly-packed current events stories that are widely available across the world through *The Guardian, The New York Times,* and BBC to be consumed by global citizens, young and old. This may be contributing to the mainstream normalization of the horrific acts committed by terrorist organizations and a propaganda machine that is constantly churning out content, reminding marginalized Western Muslims of the inequities in the societies in which they live. The Counter Terrorism Internet Referral Unit in the United Kingdom, which was established in 2010, removed 49,000 pieces of extremist content between 2010 and October 2014. This does not seem like much until the unit reported that 30,000 pieces of content alone had been removed between December 2013 and October 2014, of which, the majority referred to Syria and Iraq.

In terms of the Islamic State, while a majority of their members are located within Iraq and Syria, through using the internet to craft a global network of what U.S. intelligence officials deem as a *small unit within IS [that] is leading the group's cyber ambitions, which range from working with hackers to launch cyber attacks against their enemies, to publishing manuals that help their supporters mask their online communication and defend themselves from those hunting them (Frenkel, 2016).*

The issues with IS and their use of the internet for terroristic purposes become more complicated because the group, like the web itself, is ever-evolving and becoming more sophisticated users of tools like encryption, malware to take down sites that are attempting to expose the atrocities of IS to Muslims, and a standard favorite of hacktivists and terrorists alike, denial-of-service (DDoS) attacks. Not only are terrorist groups becoming more technologically savvy, the younger demographic allows for the swift adoption of new platforms from across the globe that aid in the communication.

A recent study found that the median age of the world's 1.6 billion Muslims is 23-years old (Talbot, 2015), making them within the first "digital generation" (Alder, 2013), a generation that has never not known what it was like without the internet or digital technologies. The dominance of IS by younger members does help the group take advantage of newer applications or platforms before governments catch on. For example, the Berlin-based messaging application known as Telegram has become a popular tool for Islamic State followers. In October 2015, use of Telegram spiked among IS supporters with nearly 9,000 users following the IS channel in less than a week (Russon, 2016), and the founders Nikolai and Pavel Durov noted at a TechCrunch panel that privacy is more crucial than fear of terrorism (Frenkel, 2016). However, Telegram did eventually suspend "78 public Islamic State-related channels in 12 languages" (Russon, 2016).

Terror groups are using photo-sharing services such as Instagram as a means to relate with younger recruits and sympathizers, most of whom are within the digital generation and consume information visually just as much as they do textually. Instagram allows IS members to showcase their battles, their conception of the utopian caliphate and provide details into the daily life of an IS member, helping to normalize their actions to new recruits (Vitale & Keagle, 2014). Applications such as Ask.fm and KIK are both aimed at teenage-use and are used by IS to assist in answering questions anonymously. The anonymity is crucial to Western users who may be interested in joining the jihadist movement but do not know how to begin the process. These applications assist by linking the possible recruit to a member who can provide them with answers to lure them into participation.

IS supporters are also in the business of creating applications and platforms, such as Alwari, which operates on an Android system. Alwari was created to ensure that communications between IS supporters would remain secure, as reported by Ghost Security Group (GhostSec), a counterterrorism hacktivist organization (Russon, 2016). This is not the first application that was IS-devised either. Kingsley reports (2014), the Palestinian affiliate of the Islamic State created the Dawn of Glad Tidings application with assistance and approval from leaders in Iraq and Syria. At the peak of its popularity Dawn of Glad Tidings "posted 40,000 tweets in a single day from the battlefield using countless users' accounts" (Vitale & Kegale, 2014, Pg. 7). The application

allows IS to use their accounts to send out centrally written updates....the messages swamp social media, giving IS a far larger online reach than their own accounts would otherwise allow (Kingsley, 2014).

Hackers with numerous pro-Islamic State groups, including the United Cyber Caliphate (UCC) have made the work of Western governments working to dismantle the communication structure of jihadism to a new level. The UCC has published a 'kill list' that contained the names and personal identification of more than 40 U.S. government employees whose jobs encompass national security and counterterrorism. The Cyber Caliphate Army is another hacker group that has pledged allegiance to the Islamic State who also released a 'kill list' of American officials, and threatened "Electronic War" on the U.S. and Europe (Masi, 2015). The Islamic State Hacking Division has leaked personal information of nearly 100 members of the U.S. military and invited IS supporters to find and kill them (Dunham & Beech, 2015). Mikko Hypponen, cyber security expert noted in 2015 that the Islamic State has the technological capabilities to conduct a major infrastructural attack on the West (Yadron, 2015). This is coming at a particularly vulnerable time for U.S. digital infrastructure as international actors such as China and Russia have exposed not only civilian data and information, but also government officials and employees. If the Islamic State is paying attention to the U.S. presidential campaign during Summer 2016, and the hacks of party apparatus servers or state voter registration databases, the U.S. cyber landscape can be compromised, leaving the door open for more than just theft of data.

Beyond social media platforms and mobile applications, major technological actors like Google are weighing free speech and content on their search engine. The company noted in May 2016 that more than 50,000 people search for the phrase 'join IS' every month (Frenkel, 2016), and when one completes the search, one can find most of the information necessary to join the organization, as well as their ideological content that inspires attacks globally. Zelin (2015) emphasizes the breadth of the Islamic State's media apparatus in his study of one week's (April 18-24, 2015) media releases from the group, the group indeed conducts much of their communication via the internet and social media. However, they have established numerous media "wings" that include its news agency, A'maq and radio station al-Bayan (Pg. 88). According to Zelin's analysis, al-Bayan Radio Station characterizes IS military fronts, advances, and achievements daily (2015, Pg. 90). While the radio station's broadcast area remains secluded to Iraq, Syria and Libya, the news/talk radio format is broadcast in Kurdish, Arabic, English, French, and Russian languages (Sharma, 2015). The Islamic State releases segments of broadcasts featuring military advances on Twitter in various languages for mass consumption, adding yet another level to their ability to influence.

OUTSOURCING TERRORISM

Transference of tactics to other established terror organizations that are not (or initially were not) affiliated with the Islamic State have attempted to mimic their social media and digital campaign to increase membership. Groups such as Boko Haram, a Nigerian-based terrorist organization began borrowing from the Islamic State tactics in 2014, taking their strategy of conquering lands and made claims of establishing a caliphate (Youssef, 2015). Boko Haram was established in 2002 but did not begin military operations until 2009 in northern Nigeria. The group came into international awareness when it abducted at least 200 schoolgirls in April 2014, which led to the #BringBackOurGirls campaign via social media whose participants included United States First Lady Michelle Obama (Ross, 2016). In January 2015, the group established their online presence with a media channel, The *Indissoluble Link* that appeared similar to the Islamic State's *Furqan* channel. The Indissoluble Link also created a Twitter profile that was immediately publicized by IS supporters (Youssef, 2015). The adoption and streamlining of Boko Haram's social media and propaganda campaign suggested to many in the international community that the group was receiving assistance from the Islamic State or wanted to legitimize themselves with the Islamic State in order for cooperation to take place.

According to Zellin (Youssef, 2015), "For Boko Haram, working with the Islamic State bolsters its legitimacy and could potentially help it gain recruits and funding." According to a *New York Times* article from April 2016, Boko Haram and IS are cooperating more since the former pledged allegiance to the latter in March 2015, citing a convoy of seized weapons on route to the Lake Chad region believed to have originated with the Islamic State in Libya, which provides evidence that the organizations are cooperating (Cooper, 2016). The intercontinental coordination of terrorism is as much of a consequence of the internet and digital media as increased transparency and democracy in the West.

Although terrorism beyond IS, particularly when discussing Al Qaeda, has become more localized in recent years (Berger, 2015) – the digital precedent set by IS has led to significant alliances for the group in their spread of not only ideology, but in physical space. The United States, launched in August 2016, an airstrike campaign against IS in Libya in the stronghold of Sirte (Ackerman et al., 2016); it is widely known that Tunisia is a major exporter of terrorists who are sympathetic to the IS cause (Trofimov, 2016); and Egypt has been fighting the group in the Sinai Peninsula since 2014 (Cunningham, 2014). The advancement of IS in the Middle East and Northern Africa (MENA) region, which includes the physical occupation of land, utilities, and geopolitical resources as well as the effective spread of the ideological mission has resulted in a multi-continental conflict. This conflict includes Western countries that seek to destroy the Islamic State at its roots without considering their language and message that continues to resonate. This global resonance that has manifested into inspired or coordinated attacks is possible thanks to the leveling of the communications structure on the part of the Islamic State. It is through "direct, real-time, and independently targeted engagements [that IS] formulate and solidify group loyalties around jihadist messages that enact moral and religious responsibilities" (Bjelopera, 2013, Pg. 18).

As of 2016, there are more than 50 international organizations that have pledged allegiance or *bay'at* to the Islamic State, making an extension of the group in their region, which now includes Egypt, Libya, Tunisia, Chechnya, Uzbekistan, and Tajikistan (Day, 2016). This expansion of IS ideology to the MENA region has presented numerous challenges to Western governments who would like to militarily quell the spread of IS ideology and political theatre, but also threatens the stability of fragile Arab Spring nations who have yet to rebuild stable governments. Many of the groups pledging allegiance are focused on local or regional issues as opposed to the global jihadist movement. This is particularly interesting if the Islamic State is going to sustain those international alliances when they are predicated on localized issues. Although the future of the stratified Islamic State structure is to be determined, the short-term gains and projection of strength in numbers does aid in the perception of their organization's resiliency.

IS has taken advantage of the digital media environment's lack of structure when it comes to communication, offering a non-hierarchical, horizontal, and decentralized means to share content. While it is critical to not overstate the importance of digital media, that is to say, traditional networks of communication, namely the family and other foundational aspects of a community (media, churches/mosques, etc.) remain crucial pieces of radicalization, the internet and accompanying tools have supplemented and enhanced traditional networks as well as opening the jihadist network to millions who would have not had access to it as readily in the pre-digital era. Michael Steinbach, Assistant Director of the Federal Bureau of Investigation, noted in testimony before the U.S. House Committee on Homeland Security that the Islamic State's use of horizontal media distribution "allows direct access to spot, assess, recruit, and radicalize" via the internet, something that no other terror organization before had attempted to do (Steinbach, 2015).

The IS media strategy provides for personalization and a recruiter being able to customize the message in order to appeal to individuals using various types of content, from the vicious beheading and killing videos to memes featuring kittens to attract young women theoretically. The Islamic State has mastered using both *hard power* (military fronts and inspired and/or coordinated attacks) as well as *soft power* (communication of religious and political utopianism in the creation of the Caliphate), which has been quite effective thus far not only in recruitment but confusing oppositional tactics for fighting back. For example, as Twitter account suspensions for users dedicated to the Islamic State began to destabilize the group's network, which hit 235,000 suspensions in August 2016 (Flores & Brennan, 2016), IS methodically shifted their social media use from user-centric (profiles associated with or belonging to known IS members) content dissemination to a hashtag-driven model, which further decentralizes their messages making it hard to pin down to a single individual user profile (Glavin, 2015).

The following chapter will focus on the difficulties that Western governments are having in challenging Islamic State rhetoric and their swift spread of ideology that has served to inspire a multitude of attacks around the world. The threat of IS is occurring at a peculiar time for global relations, as we are seeing a trend in many Western societies turning away from the globalism and integration that defined the post-modern era toward nationalism, or rebuilding of a strong national identity while eschewing international brands, values, and norms. This move inward could be a very dangerous detriment to the collective international response to the Islamic State, as more nations are taking disparate measures to counter terrorism within their borders (i.e.: immigration and/or refugee policies), yet there is not an evident coordinated global effort to combat the spread of extremist ideology via digital tools.

REFERENCES

Ackerman, S., Stephen, C., & MacAskill, E. (2016, Aug. 1). US launches airstrikes against ISIS in Libya. *The Guardian.* Retrieved from https://www.theguardian.com/world/2016/aug/01/us-airstrikes-against-isis-libya-pentagon

Alder, J. (2013, April 16). Meet the First Digital Generation. Now Get Ready to Play by Their Rules. *Wired.* Retrieved from https://www.wired.com/2013/04/genwired/

Arquilla, J., & Ronfeldt, D., & Zanini, M. (2000, April). Information-Age Terrorism. *Current History (New York, N.Y.)*, *99*(636), 179–185.

Bakker, E., & de Graaf, B. (2011). Preventing Lone Wolf Terrorism: some CT Approaches Addressed. *Perspectives on Terrorism, 5*(5-6).

Berger, J. M. (2015, March 6). *The ISIS Twitter census: Making sense of ISIS's use of Twitter*. Brookings Institute. Retrieved from https://www.brookings.edu/blog/order-from-chaos/2015/03/06/the-isis-twitter-census-making-sense-of-isiss-use-of-twitter/

Bergin. (2008, April 5). Facebook terrorism investigation. *The Advertiser.*

Bjelopera, J. P. (2013). American Jihadist Terrorism: Combating a Complex Threat. *Congressional Research Service.* Retrieved from https://www.fas.org/sgp/crs/terror/R41416.pdf

Brooking, E., & Singer, P. W. (2016, Nov.). War goes Viral. *The Atlantic.* Retrieved from http://www.theatlantic.com/magazine/archive/2016/11/war-goes-viral/501125/

Conway, M. (2006). Terrorism and the Internet: New Media- New Threat? *Parliamentary Affairs*, *59*(2), 283–298. doi:10.1093/pa/gsl009

Cooper, H. (2016, April 20). Boko Haram and ISIS are collaborating more, U.S. military says. *New York Times.* Retrieved from http://www.nytimes.com/2016/04/21/world/africa/boko-haram-and-isis-are-collaborating-more-us-military-says.html

Cunningham, E. (2014, Oct. 24). Bomb blast in Egypt's Sinai Peninsula is deadliest attack on army in decades. *Washington Post.* Retrieve from https://www.washingtonpost.com/world/bomb-attack-in-egypts-sinai-peninsula-is-deadliest-attack-on-its-army-in-years/2014/10/24/98d14ad7-91c0-4acd-835f-e61b8f18a434_story.html

Day, J. (2016, March). *The ISIS Bandwagon: Under What Conditions Do Groups Pledge Support?* Boston University Institute on Culture, Religion, and World Affairs. Retrieved from https://www.bu.edu/cura/files/2016/03/The-ISIS-Bandwagon-V3.pdf

Dewey, C. (2015, Nov. 23). The secret American origins of Telegram, the encrypted messaging app favored by the Islamic State. *The Washington Post.* Retrieved from https://www.washingtonpost.com/news/the-intersect/wp/2015/11/23/the-secret-american-origins-of-telegram-the-encrypted-messaging-app-favored-by-the-islamic-state/

Dunham, W., & Beech, E. (2015, March 21). Islamic State calls on backers to kill 100 U.S. military personnel. *Reuters.* Retrieved from http://www.reuters.com/article/us-mideast-crisis-threat-idUSKBN0MH0QQ20150321

Flores, R., & Brennan, M. (2016, Aug. 18). Twitter announces it has suspended 235,000 terror-linked accounts. *CBS News.* Retrieved from http://www.cbsnews.com/news/twitter-announces-it-has-suspended-235000-terror-linked-accounts/

Frenkel, S. (2016, May 12). This is How ISIS uses the Internet. *Buzzfeed News.* Retrieved from https://www.buzzfeed.com/sheerafrenkel/everything-you-ever-wanted-to-know-about-how-isis-uses-the-i?utm_term=.jr0AjwPE5#.vseo9gxq2

Frontline. (2014). *The Rise of ISIS.* Retrieved from http://www.pbs.org/wgbh/frontline/film/rise-of-isis/

Gibbons-Neff, T. (2016, Oct. 11). ISIS used an armed drone to kill two Kurdish fighters and wound French troops, report says. *The Washington Post.* Retrieved from https://www.washingtonpost.com/news/checkpoint/wp/2016/10/11/isis-used-an-armed-drone-to-kill-two-kurdish-fighters-and-wound-french-troops-report-says/

Glavin, N. (2015, Dec. 7). Counter ISIS' Narratives on Social Media. *The New York Times.* Retrieved from http://www.nytimes.com/roomfordebate/2015/12/06/how-can-america-counter-the-appeal-of-isis/counter-isis-narratives-on-social-media

Hammadi, S., Scammell, R., & Yuhas, A. (2016, July 3). Dhaka cafe attack ends with 20 hostages among dead. *The Guardian.* Retrieved from https://www.theguardian.com/world/2016/jul/01/dhaka-bangladesh-restaurant-attack-hostages

Hegel, G. W. F., & Miller, A. V. (1977). Force and the Understanding: Appearance and the Supersensible World: Phenomenology of Spirit (5th ed.). New York: Oxford University Press.

Hussain, G., & Saltman, E. (2014). Jihad Trending: A Comprehensive Analysis of Online Extremism and How to Counter It. *Quilliam.* Retrieved from https://www.quilliamfoundation.org/wp/wp-content/uploads/publications/free/jihad-trending-quilliam-report.pdf

Jasparro, C. (2010). *Lone Wolf – The Threat from Independent Jihadists.* Retrieved from https://wikileaks.org/gifiles/attach/168/168290_Osac-jir1209.pdf

Jenkins, B. M. (2006). *The New Age of Terrorism.* RAND Corporation. Retrieved from http://www.rand.org/content/dam/rand/pubs/reprints/2006/RAND_RP1215.pdf

Kam, E. (2015). The Islamic State Surprise: The Intelligence Perspective. *Strategic Assessment*, *18*(3), 21–31.

Kingsley, P. (2014, June 23). Who is behind ISIS's terrifying online propaganda operation? *The Guardian.* Retrieved from https://www.theguardian.com/world/2014/jun/23/who-behind-isis-propaganda-operation-iraq

Koerner, B. (2016, June 12). The Orlando Nightclub Shooting could have been an ISIS plan with ISIS knowing nothing about it. *Wired.* Retrieved from https://www.wired.com/2016/06/orlando-massacre-shows-isis-outsources-terror/

Masi, A. (2015, May 11). ISIS-Affiliated Hackers Threaten Cyberattacks, 'Electronic War' on US, Europe. *International Business Times.* Retrieved from http://www.ibtimes.com/isis-affiliated-hackers-threaten-cyberattacks-electronic-war-us-europe-1917320

Newman, L. (2016, June 8). France releases terror alert app. *Slate*. Retrieved from http://www.slate.com/blogs/future_tense/2016/06/08/france_releases_terror_alert_app.html

Ross, W. (2016, May 18). Chibok girls: Kidnapped schoolgirl found in Nigeria. *BBC News*. Retrieved from http://www.bbc.com/news/world-africa-36321249

Russon, M. (2016, Jan. 14). Alrawi: ISIS has built secure Android messaging app to replace Telegram, says Anonymous affiliate GhostSec. *International Business Times*. Retrieved from http://www.ibtimes.co.uk/alrawi-isis-builds-secure-android-messaging-app-replace-telegram-says-anonymous-affiliate-ghostsec-1537948

Sharma, S. (2015, June 4). Islamic State has an English-language radio broadcast that sounds eerily like NPR. *The Washington Post*. Retrieved from https://www.washingtonpost.com/news/worldviews/wp/2015/06/04/islamic-state-has-a-daily-english-language-radio-broadcast-that-sounds-eerily-like-it-could-be-on-npr/

Soriano, M. (2008). Terrorism and the Mass Media after Al Qaeda: A Change of Course? *Athena Intelligence Journal*, *3*(1), 1–20.

Spaaij, R. (2010). The Enigma of Lone Wolf Terrorism: An Assessment. *Studies in Conflict and Terrorism*, *33*(9), 854–870. doi:10.1080/1057610X.2010.501426

Starr, B. (2016, Sept. 13). US bombs ISIS chemical weapons plant. *CNN News*. Retrieved from http://www.cnn.com/2016/09/13/politics/isis-chemical-weapons-plant/

Steinbach, M. (2015, June 3). *Terrorism Gone Viral: The Attack in Garland, Texas and Beyond*. Federal Bureau of Investigations. Statement before the House Homeland Security Committee. Retrieved from https://www.fbi.gov/news/testimony/terrorism-gone-viral-the-attack-in-garland-texas-and-beyond

Stern, J. (2003). *Terror in the Name of God: Why Religious Militants Kill*. New York: HarperCollins.

Talbot, D. (2015, Sept. 30). Fighting ISIS Online. *MIT Technology Review*. Retrieved from https://www.technologyreview.com/s/541801/fighting-isis-online/

Teich, S. (2013, Oct.). Trends and Developments in Lone Wolf Terrorism in the Western World. *International Institute for Counter-Terrorism.* Retrieved from http://www.ctcitraining.org/docs/LoneWolf_SarahTeich2013.pdf

Torok, R. (2013). Developing an explanatory model for the process of online radicalization and terrorism. Perth, Australia: Springer. Retrieved from http://www.security-informatics.com/content/2/1/6

Trofimov, Y. (2016, Sept. 9). What Happens After ISIS Falls? *The Wall Street Journal.* Retrieved from http://www.wsj.com/articles/what-happens-after-isis-falls-1473435007

Trofimov, Y. (2016, Feb. 25). How Tunisia Became a Top Source of ISIS Recruits. *The Wall Street Journal.* Retrieved from http://www.wsj.com/articles/how-tunisia-became-a-top-source-of-isis-recruits-1456396203

Tuysuz, G., & Almasy, S. (2016, July 6). Istanbul airport explosions: 36 dead, 147 injured, Turkish officials say. *CNN News.* Retrieved from http://www.cnn.com/2016/06/28/europe/turkey-istanbul-airport-attacks/

Vitale, H. M., & Keagle, J. M. (2014). A time to tweet, as well as a time to kill: ISIS's projection of power in Iraq and Syria. *Defense Horizons,* (77). Retrieved from http://search.proquest.com/docview/1618549256?accountid=8289

Weimann, G. (2014). New Terrorism and New Media. Washington, DC: Commons Lab of the Woodrow Wilson International Center for Scholars. Retrieved from https://www.wilsoncenter.org/sites/default/files/STIP_140501_new_terrorism_F.pdf

Wieviorka, M. (2004). *The making of Terrorism.* Chicago: The University of Chicago Press.

Wire Staff, C. N. N. (2012, May 23). U.S. senators: Al Qaeda calls for 'electronic jihad'. *CNN.* Retrieved from http://www.cnn.com/2012/05/23/politics/al-qaeda-electronic-jihad/

Yadron, D. (2015, Oct. 20). Free Services Make the Internet a Privacy Nightmare, Security Researcher Says. *Wall Street Journal.* Retrieved from http://www.wsj.com/articles/free-services-make-the-internet-a-privacy-nightmare-security-researcher-says-1445370168

Youssef, N. (2015, Jan. 29). ISIS and Boko Haram's Unholy Online Alliance. *The Daily Beast.* Retrieved from http://www.thedailybeast.com/articles/2015/01/29/isis-and-boko-haram-s-unholy-online-alliance.html

Zelin, A. (2015). Picture Or It Didn't Happen: A Snapshot of the Islamic State's Official Media Output. *Perspectives on Terrorism, 9*(4). Retrieved from http://www.terrorismanalysts.com/pt/index.php/pot/article/view/445/html

Chapter 3
Delayed Governance?

INTRODUCTION

In the midst of writing this book, as stated previously, the global community has endured a harsh summer, with IS attacks spanning the globe and throughout May, June, and July 2016. The fear of terrorism and the projection of strength on behalf of the Islamic State have permeated Western societies. A Gallup poll released in December 2015 revealed that half of the Americans surveyed were "somewhat" or "very worried" that terrorism would affect a family member (Swift, 2015). Similarly in Great Britain, 74 percent of participants in a 2015 poll believed a terrorist attack in their country was imminent (Apps, 2015), and 60 percent of people in a German poll believe that the influx of refugees is more than the country can sustain (*The Daily Express*, 2016). In summary, the Western world has taken heed of the Islamic State, which has diligently worked to expose more citizens around the world to their ideology and goals through both digital communication as well as the terrorist stand-by of coordinating and inspiring attacks.

DOI: 10.4018/978-1-5225-2190-7.ch003

On August 4, U.S. President Obama gave his first update on the fight against IS since June 2016, directly following the lone wolf attack on Orlando nightclub Pulse. Notably, Obama acknowledged (as he has in the past with still too few details) that it would take "more than military strength alone to defeat IS", that this fight was as much ideological as it was physical. Yet he did not mention what the U.S. is doing in terms of combating the continued and swift dissemination of extremist propaganda, particularly as it pertains to online efforts. Perhaps it would have divulged too much national security and counterterrorism tactics to the perceived enemy (ies), but there is an international academic and foreign policy community that is witnessing, as Obama himself noted, a group that is losing on the military front but as they are losing physical ground, are gaining in recruitment, mobilization and inspiration of more frequent, smaller-scale attacks carried out by individuals or small cells.

MILITARY TACTICS

The United States' military engagement to limit the Islamic State's physical sphere of influence will not be enough to dismantle the foundation of the group, which lies within its ability to publicize the jihad and advances online to the masses. In September 2014, General James Clapper, Director of National Intelligence conceded that the United States had failed to recognize the strength of the Islamic State in relation to the weakness of the Iraqi army and unwillingness of the Syrian regime to fight IS with the force that the regime was fighting the rebel faction attempting to take out the Assad regime. Clapper stated, "What we didn't do was predict the Islamic State's will to fight…In this case, we underestimated IS, and overestimated the fighting capability of the Iraqi army (Ignatius, 2014).

As Vitale and Keagle (2014) argue, the United States must take an aggressive role in counteracting the spread of powerful propaganda by IS by waging a "proactive digital campaign" as opposed to the continued reactive foreign policy that has long plagued the Obama administration. The existence of a multitude of social media platforms and IS-managed, supported, or inspired accounts is an advantage to global intelligence agencies, but particularly the United States, where many of the most popular sites originate and are maintained. It is crucial that Western governments wage an aggressive digital attack on the communication and recruitment operations of IS, as well as the actual construction of a coalition of Middle Eastern nations willing to speak out and 'put boots on the ground' to dismantle the group's logistical headquarters in Iraq and Syria.

The international coalition that President Obama called upon to respond to the threat of the Islamic State in his September 2014 'degrade and destroy' speech to the nation manifested as 62 countries pledging support, including 10 regional nations such as Oman, Qatar, United Arab Emirates, Bahrain, Kuwait, Saudi Arabia, and Turkey (Drennen, 2014). Yet the Islamic State was a much different enemy than terrorist groups faced in the past; the organization integrated themselves amongst the populations captured along with the territory, making it more difficult to justify an all-out invasion. Another contentious factor that impeded the response of the U.S. against the Islamic State was the almost immediate attachment of the terror organization to the fight against President Bashar Assad in Syria, meaning that fighting the Islamic State now meant also involving Western militaries in the now five years long civil war on the ground in Syria.

A major obstacle to the physical reprisal against the Islamic State in the region they occupy is the Western relationship with Turkey, which will be only briefly mentioned, the subject itself warrants an additional volume of research. The battle for the border town of Kobani against the Islamic State was a major test for alliances between the U.S. and Turkey. The Turkish military, however, did not engage or send troops into Syria to fight alongside a predominately Kurdish military force, and refused to allow coalition jets to use the U.S. airbase in Incirlik to reach targets in Syria more efficiently.

The early Kobani display by the Turkish government and military forces threw into question if the U.S. would be able to trust its Middle East coalition to truly assert military strength in the battle against IS. Turkey has maintained a "largely porous border" at its southern end, leading into northern Syria, which is currently an IS stronghold (Vitale & Keagle, 2014, Pg. 10). French military intelligence officials estimate that 100 foreigners continue to enter Syria to fight with IS from Turkey (Reuters, 2016). The politics of modern Turkey have moved incrementally toward a less secular society under the direction of President Recep Tayyip Erdogan, whose regime suffered an international scandal with the Gezi Park protests in the first year of the presidency in 2014. This indifference by the Turkish regime to seal off its southern perimeter and disallow IS recruits a main route to Syria remains a source of contention for the United States, which perceive Erdogan as capitulating to a more powerful enemy.

THE PROPAGANDA MACHINE: IS VS. THE WEST

Much of the strength of the Islamic State is garnered through perception and projections of military and ideological strength, which is effectively achieved through social media domination. Vitale and Keagle (2014) encourage the United States to counterbalance the message of IS online by using their own channels and forums against them, establishing a reality-based narrative that unveils the horrors of IS particularly to likely target Western audiences (teens, disaffected youth). The U.S. State Department created a program on Twitter that responds to users through direct messaging who tweet pro-IS/terrorist content known as "Think Again Turn Away". The aim of Think Again is to make unbiased, non-propagandized information available to potential recruits to assist them in making informed decisions regarding participation in jihadist activities. Yet the program, as stated, is reactive – depending on administrators catching the pro-jihadist message and properly identifying statistics or evidence negating the content, as well as the user being open to receiving a government-sanctioned truth.

In 2011, President Barack Obama established the Center for Strategic Counterterrorism Communications (CSCC) with a Digital Outreach Team that disseminates targeted tweets to Al Qaeda supporters. The group oversaw the Think Again program that operated as a government-sponsored trolling venture, which is not an effective means to counter the ideological and utopian messages that the Islamic State is selling its supporters. The CSCC did create a remarkably effective video entitled "Welcome to ISIS land" that went viral in 2015, which was viewed over 844,000 times on YouTube, and provided a good juxtaposition of ISIS atrocities against Muslims in the Middle East as part of the jihad (Miller & Higham, 2015). However, engaging in social media battles with the enemy is no way to combat the spread of hateful content – in other words, fighting hate with hate is proving to only fan the fires of jihadism rather than offering real alternatives and inclusion in society for Muslims worldwide.

The Think Again program and other Western programs are necessary in the fight against the spread of IS and jihadist ideology online, which threatens the future of the international community. According to a report released by Fordham University's Center on National Security in July 2016, since 2014, 100 people have been arrested on charges related to supplying the Islamic State with support (which is vaguely defined). In 69 percent of the cases, "officials found the individuals had watched or read the group's electronic dispatches" (Hong, 2016).

It is worth noting the importance of how the messaging, particularly state-sponsored messaging is conceptualized and perceived by the target population, Muslim youth. Reactions to the various terrorist events in the West by both governments and civilians has led to more volatile societies as well as increased tensions between Muslims and non-Muslims. The decision by the French government to ban hijab in 2004, following the September 11, 2001 attack, as well as the introduction of the Burqa ban in 2011 have led Muslims living in French society to feel disenfranchised. Most recently, French officials attempted to pass a ban on the 'burkini,' a modest alternative to a traditional bathing suit, which includes a fitted version of the hijab, after the Bastille Day attack on Nice (2016). In the United States, presidential candidate Donald Trump has proposed a fairly reactionary plan to ban all Muslims from entering the country without "extreme vetting" and possibly the administration of a religious test. These types of hostile reactions, which generalize all Muslims as terrorists are extremely dangerous and counterintuitive to the elimination of IS messages of a utopia for the disaffected global Muslim population. Hong (2016) notes, "Experts widely acknowledge that directives from the U.S. government are unlikely to resonate with young people interested in joining the Islamic State."

Vitale and Keagle recommend the State Department adapt Think Again into a proactive program that targets the same audience to "subtly promote Western values and efforts" and "could be enhance[d] through the use of frank photos and depictions of dead jihadists by creating memes that could go viral" (2014, Pg. 11). Seemingly, a more proactive approach to the digital front on the part of global state entities, and certainly targeting the same audience and flooding known IS channels of communication with messages of violent and visceral images of the realities of waging jihad could be productive in curbing the massive flow of Western Muslims to the IS battlefront. It would, however, fly in the face of promotion of democratic values to post and promote death in the social media space as a means to counter the narrative of IS death and destruction.

In particular, a message or theme that furthers a violently aggressive campaign against mainly Muslim actors could only exacerbate existing tensions in Western societies, and in effect creating more terrorists than eliminating the potential for radicalization. A more effective means of capturing the attention of the target audience could be partnering with more pervasive brands such as Marvel Comics, who own the rights to Captain America or Home Box Office (HBO), who produce the globally popular Game of Thrones television series to create content to negate the impact of IS's ideological campaign. Digital researchers recognize the co-option of content in order to send a message, mainly done through the use of GIFs (graphics interchange format) or memes, typically photos, videos, or texts that are effectively passed from one individual to another within a culture (or subculture).

This co-option could be more strategically used by government officials in coordination with elements of national or global popular culture to send the same message to potential recruits around the world who are likely to be engaged with the content on its own (consumption of television shows or movies). As Vitale and Keagle note, "The United States must be as nimble, if not more nimble, than IS's communications arm to deter and attract would-be jihadists from deploying to Syria", or more importantly today, from being inspired by group and committing lone wolf attacks (2014, Pg. 11).

The Think Again Program amply highlights a problem that exists within the international community as it pertains to counterterrorism efforts, mainly that these programs are too often stratified and reach users within their society. But there are not enough resources devoted to cyber-alliances, cooperation among national programs, or nearly enough officials within one nation to combat the entirety of IS (and other terrorist groups' communication on a daily basis). This will be addressed further in the next chapter as a suggestion to government entities to establish more stable allegiances with non-governmental organizations and hacktivist groups.

The U.S. government has stepped up its encouragement of civil society and private sector members to become involved in counterterrorism online. Facebook, for example, received help from the government in establishing competitions for global college students to create personal counterterrorism campaigns, in Spring 2016 there were 54 universities participating (Hong, 2016).

COUNTERTERRORISM: GOVERNMENT AND CORPORATE

As the United States witnessed in the aftermath of the attack on a San Bernardino medical and business complex by a married couple in 2015, issues of right to privacy, corporate responsibility, and terrorism investigations provide an intriguing spectacle. The internet creates new challenges for governments and law enforcement to develop counterterrorism measures that are up-to-date not only with the terror groups and their goals, but also their tactics and tools of choice, including now an increased focus on the digital. Berger and Strathearn (2013, Pg. 41) note that for technology and social media companies, "Freedom of speech is not synonymous with the freedom to use a specific company's services." This translates to Twitter, Facebook, and Google have the right to remove content and block and/or suspend users who violate the terms of service as agreed to and amended by the corporation, not based around the fundamental values of freedom of speech in a political sense or a right in most Western countries.

So at the moment, the burden falls on the social media company to determine what the line is between free expression and what constitutes an actual threat to the safety of people in the real world. Members of the British Parliament (MP) accused social media giants, Facebook, Twitter and YouTube of "consciously failing" to halt the spread of jihadist and extremist propaganda via their websites (Travis, 2016). Although Twitter did recently report the successful closure of more than 235,000 accounts for promulgating terrorist messages, the MPs are not convinced that the suspensions would have much of an effect (as noted previously, IS has been migrating its conversations and propaganda-spreading from individual user accounts to a more stratified strategy of hashtag-utilization, which makes it much harder for companies or law enforcement to pinpoint the originating account).

Berger argues that social media companies like Twitter can aid further in fleshing out digital jihadists by allowing social scientists an opportunity to analyze the data behind suspended accounts, as well as writing more transparent guidelines regarding the type of content that can lead to a suspension. Berger adds that Twitter has become a crucial tool for political and social scientists who can glean much information from metadata and API, stating "ISIS broadly telegraphed its intention to declare itself a "caliphate" on Twitter months in advance of the actual announcement. Twitter also allowed me to see, very early, that key Al Qaeda supporters were defecting to IS. More recently, Twitter activity showed the Boko Haram was getting ready to establish a more formal relationship with ISIS" (Berger, 2015). Thus, the activity that is available to be surveilled is vast and suspension of accounts may lead to less information for law enforcement and counterterrorism experts to analyze and pinpoint emerging threats.

The Online Hate Prevention Institute, a group based in Australia that fights online hate speech and discrimination, have pressured Facebook to update their reporting system, such as increased automation and IP address-based bans. Yet in the U.S. corporate environment and its tenuous relationship with the government, the question exists, is it the corporations' responsibility to employ thousands of monitors to counter the language of extremism, terrorism, sexism, etc.? According to Brooking and Singer (2016),

The convergence of online speech and physical violence creates new dilemmas not only for nations, but also for the companies that created and are now responsible for the digital landscape.

This author believes the corporation does play some role in countering the narrative on the platform they provide for all, in an egalitarian manner, yet it should not rise to the level of censorship. This becomes a very fine line to walk. A program that rises to the level of unconstitutional, warrantless surveillance of American citizens would play into the hands of IS, particularly if that program targeted law-abiding American-Muslim citizens. This would further prove the Islamic State's assertion that Muslims will never be accepted in the West in order to manipulate recruits into loyalty to the utopian caliphate. Some experts argue that surveillance and suspension of accounts should be based on the content posted and not the group to which it is promoting, as a way to avoid base discrimination against one demographic or another, think Black Lives Matter protestors versus Islamic State proponents. If the focus is on a group, the line of free speech and discrimination can be blurred quickly. But then the question for governments and the civil society is what content is too much (bloody, gruesome, inciting rage mobilization, sexist, racist, etc.)?

The relationship between social media/technological corporations, the civil society, and government must be more clearly defined as we move forward into more advanced digital warfare, which now encompasses spreading ideology as much as it does hacking and cyber attacks against another country. In 2016, Facebook has the power to manipulate the tone of news its users are receiving as 'trending', and thus has the ability to bias its 1.7 billion-member user base toward one solution, political party, policy, nation or another. At some point, the global community must recognize that major social media corporations (Twitter, Facebook) do affect politics and the actions of political actors, and work to not censor content, but find a balance between being a benign communication platform and an effective and formidable sociopolitical influencer. As Zeynep Tufecki (2016) noted in *The New York Times,* "What we are shown is shaped by these algorithms, which are shaped by what the companies want from us, and there is nothing neutral about that," so then why are consumers and the government so keen on treating these platforms as observers as opposed to participants?

As cyber terrorism expert, Evan Kholmann (2005) notes, "Ninety percent of terrorist activity on the internet takes place using social networking tools", so what are Western governments doing to counter the vast array of propaganda that exists in the cyber realm? Current examples of national laws and counterterrorism efforts include Canada's Bill C-51 that works to identify and remove jihadist propaganda from computers and online platforms. Bill C-51 allows the Canadian Security and Intelligence Service (CSIS) to engage in counter-messaging online through, for example, accessing recruiters' Twitter accounts (Mastracci, 2015). Punishment for persons participating in or communicating any "writing, sign, visible representation or audio recording" that promotes terrorist activities includes up to five years in prison (Bill C-51, 2015). There are also amendments that have been proposed to the Criminal Code that would allow judges to order the seizure and removal of terrorist propaganda when in electronic form and disseminated via a Canadian internet service provider.

Most observers of post-9/11 legislation are aware of the United States' Patriot Act, which widely expanded law enforcement and judicial authority in the name of national security at the risk of hindering or outright eliminating personal liberties. Under 18 United States Code (U.S.C.) sections 2339A and 2339B, officials are able to prosecute citizens with providing material support to terrorists, which include a broad range of assistance that includes housing, training, and providing expert intelligence or advice. The law was strengthened under 2015's USA Freedom Act, which increased the penalty for providing such material support as the court proves from 15 to 20 years in prison. Yet the harsher sentence does not seem to be deterring jihadist ideology from spreading across the internet via Western social media platforms daily. As the U.S. has seen with its "War on Drugs" often imposing harsher punishments for vague or minor infractions (comparatively speaking to murder, rape, etc.) can lead to overcrowded prisons instead of addressing the behavior leading to crime and feelings of marginalization. In the case of supporting or pledging allegiance to terror organizations, the United States must understand that it is not simply a game of putting threats in prison, it is a psychological and ideological game that must be waged carefully in order to preserve its own citizens.

There are numerous acts in the U.S. related to the seizure of communications such as the Communications Assistance for Law Enforcement Act (1994), which allows law enforcement officials and entities to intercept telephone data but has not been extended to most internet communication. This hole in the ability for law enforcement agencies to be able to receive data without be detected provides an advantage to supporters of IS within the U.S. Again, the issue of American citizens' right to privacy via the Fourth Amendment comes up. The Third Party Doctrine allows for the content posted to social media platforms, crudely speaking, to be traded, sold, and harvested without the knowledge of the poster. As Twitter advocates, "You are what you Tweet," a good lesson for any user but particularly those who are choosing to publicly engage with jihadist material.

In April 2015, the United States announced the first digital attack conducted by the Cyber Command on the Islamic State, and planned to use hacking and cyber weapons to destroy computer systems that are affiliated or used by the Islamic State (InfoSec, 2015). The U.S. military is harnessing the internet's potential in the same way in order to counter the message of IS in Mosul, Iraq as well as interfering with their members' ability to communicate and carry out operations. U.S. Defense Secretary Ash Carter noted in early 2016 that cyber attacks have been increased against the Islamic State, and U.S. operations have to date focused more on disruption of jihadist activities online rather than dismantling their ability to spread the message. Robert O. Work, U.S. Deputy Secretary of Defense noted that the United States is "dropping cyber-bombs, we have never done that before" (Browne & Starr, 2016).

European counterterrorism efforts began in earnest after the September 11, 2001 attacks, and the initial focus was on prevention and disrupting jihadist activities. Navarro and Villaverde (2014) analyzed the over 260 counterterrorism initiatives in the European Union, and note that the number of measures "many of which cannot be understood in isolation…which greatly hinders their development, inspire little confidence…" (Pg. 4). The implementation of counterterrorism measures is on an individual national basis and the effectiveness of the law is measured in regional or local terms instead of providing for a more cooperative network among EU members.

SUGGESTIONS TO GOVERNMENT COUNTERTERRORISM EFFORTS

The above examples are illustrative of the final point made in Chapter Two, the lack of coordination among international governments in developing reasonable punishment for sympathizers who are not an active threat, similar tactics to root out digital jihadists both within their nation and abroad (as the platforms being used are international available), and increased cooperation among intelligence and counterterrorism entities, including those in the Middle East who have a vested interest in eliminating the threat of IS. Navarro and Villaverde (2014, Pg. 1) underscore the importance of an internationally coordinated response to the challenges of counterterrorism particularly within the EU, stating

these challenges … can only be combated by actions: international cooperation, military missions or international peacekeeping interventions, which in the current geopolitical circumstances should not be trivialized by EU members.

It is important to note another development over the course of writing this book, the BREXIT vote occurring in June 2016, and has been perceived by many international relations and foreign policy experts as a major blow to globalism and the tenants of international cooperation. The divorce of Great Britain from the European Union marks a shift in national and international relationships, as the vote was framed as taking back the nation from foreigners, and increased nationalism. The future of the European Union is in question at a time when the member nations need to be more invested in their collective future, as the threat of the Islamic State looms closer, both ideologically and physically. As Europol notes, Al Qaeda and other jihadist groups continue to encourage self-organized (lone wolf) attacks within the EU that aim for as many civilian casualties possible (Special meeting of European Council, 2014 Brussels). These lone wolf or small cell cases, as articulated in the previous chapter, have become the new mode of terrorist action that is decentralized (not being directed by a leader) and are largely unpredictable (without intelligence networks honing in on threats before they occur). The consequences of these attacks are not simply loss of life or economic damage, these attacks often serve as recruitment efforts to increase radicalization and encourage similar attacks around the world.

Navarro and Villaverde (2014, Pg. 11) recommend a "holistic approach" to counterterrorism, including: an increased focus on intelligence gathering, analysis, and actions based on that intelligence; the inclusion of non-governmental organizations such as academia in the decision-making process based on intelligence; and the use of imagination in creating possible terrorist scenarios to assist in preparedness. The authors' suggestions are relevant and would certainly be useful to both national and international intelligence agencies. There is still an obvious sense of regional and national efforts overshadowing an international mission to remove the threat for the entire global community. The Islamic State is not simply a Middle Eastern or European or African threat, their existence and ability to transcend national, cultural, and racial boundaries in order to build their ranks is a threat to the world's stability, and no single nation can defeat the Islamic State on its own.

The United Nations Security Council adopted Resolution 2178 in 2014 that calls for all Member States to take "national measures to prevent terrorists from exploiting technology, communications and resources to incite support for terrorist acts" (U.N., 2014, Resolution 2178). Yet it behooves Member States to develop, not necessarily uniform, but similar tactics and legislation when dealing with the dissemination of jihadist propaganda as well as coordination of the digital effort. As Glavin concludes, "Governments must continue a constructive dialogue with partners in the information technology field [intelligence agencies] to manage and mitigate threats in the cyber domain" (2015, Pg. 9). In other words, it will take more than military might to defeat the spread of Islamic State ideology and tactics for global jihad, it will take an unprecedented effort on behalf of government, intelligence entities, experts in the field of the digital, hackers (as will be more thoroughly suggested in the following chapter), and vigilant civilians.

The government responses that have been initiated such as the Think Again program tend to be reactive, and not nearly as interactive as IS materials nor match the dedication of members to personalized recruitment via social media platforms. Yet some non-governmental organizations are moving increasingly toward individual communication with potential recruits. The London-based Institute for Strategic Dialogue began an experiment in 2015 that targeted individuals at risk of radicalization on Facebook and attempted to "steer 160 of them away" (Talbot, 2015). The Institute developed a peer-to-peer anti-extremist platform for dialogue by recruiting 10 former extremists to intervene in conversations or streams posted on Facebook. The researchers then used Facebook Graph Search to identify users whose interests, liked pages, memberships, and other associations that identified they were likely moving toward or in the process of radicalization. The former extremists used a feature on Facebook that allows users to directly contact a stranger for a price; early results showed a majority of message recipients responded, while 60 percent sustained dialogue when the initial message was neutral and showing concern for their well-being (Talbot, 2015).

While the test was a small pilot, it does indicate that governments are beginning to comprehend the severity of the digital threat from IS, and the risk of their citizens defecting to the Middle East to fight for the cause. The number of individuals who have left their homes to join IS on the battlefield reached between 27,000 – 31,000 by March 2016 (Kirk, 2016) making government response to online recruitment and radicalization, arguably the most crucial aspect of counterterrorism. The Institute also partnered with Alphabet (Google's parent company), Twitter and Facebook in 2016 to conduct experiments to better hone the most effective message to countering online extremism (Hong, 2016). The report released by the Institute notes that one factor impeding the efficacy of government messaging is that it is too broad, and needs to be customized to the audience it is attempting to reach.

The U.S. has acknowledged the role that the internet and social media platforms play in promulgating jihadist propaganda as early as August 2011, and resolved in December 2011 to "develop a separate, more comprehensive strategy for countering and preventing violent extremist online radicalization and leveraging technology to empower community resilience" (Strategic Implementation Plan, 2011, Pg. 20). Yet the digital strategy that the U.S. has implemented to counter IS rhetoric has been largely defensive, and has not provided for the construction of an effective alternate narrative that dissuades individuals from radicalization or recruitment. To most individuals observing the Islamic State and its transgressions against all humanity, the acts committed are not in the name of any deity but in horrific self-advancement, to establish the caliphate and rule the believers under Sharia law. Yet the U.S. strategy of displaying the atrocities committed by the Islamic State and its supporters around the world are often the same or similar imagery used by the group itself to promote its strength (Gartenstein-Ross, 2015).

But to thousands of people who have left their homes to join the battle in Iraq and Syria or simply joined the digital jihad, the Islamic State stands as a beacon of hope. This perversion of the terrorist ideology and mission into one of salvation must be analyzed and strategically countered in ongoing digital narratives by all international governments. In order to combat the utopianism of the IS message to many disillusioned citizens around the world, it is important that each government understand the source of the instability and discontent. Otherwise, military engagements will not begat the end of the Islamic State, it will simply displace them physically while their ideological mission will continue on the digital front via the establishment of a strong global network. As Karatzogianni (2015) succinctly asserts, it is "clear that efforts to counter IS online are missing the mark", particularly when it comes to the closure of social media accounts that can provide valuable and traceable digital footprints. The Islamic State's propaganda machine has provided the group with a sustainable digital resiliency that has become crucial to manipulating public perception in order to show strength as opposed to the recent military defeats (Tikirt, Ramadi, and most recently in September 2016, the taking of the southern Turkish border).

Nations such as Israel have recognized the opportunity for identifying potential terrorists through social media platforms like Facebook, by creating profiles of individuals who have been involved in terrorism, and "using specially developed algorithms to monitor the social media accounts of young Palestinians has yielded a list of potential suspects", sometimes allowing the government to intervene before the individual can carry out the attack (*The Economist*, 2016). This type of avid surveillance of a group of citizens may not be useful when it comes to identifying active IS members living in the West and proactively planning attacks, mainly because it is impossible to identify a likely IS member, what they should look like and how they should act.

In many of the recent lone wolf attacks, traditional networks (friends, family, churches/mosques) would have provided more insight into the radicalization of the perpetrator than online commentary. So while it is highly recommended by this author that Western governments increase their digital efforts and provide for a more comprehensive strategy for battling IS ideology online, it is also crucial for those traditional networks to also be vigilant in reporting suspicious activities, language, etc. Gartenstein-Ross (2015, Pg. 4) notes that the U.S. needs to

adapt some of its internal processes that stand in the way of competing with an organization like IS that moves at the speed of social media. The U.S.'s inefficient and highly bureaucratic internal processes often make it hard-pressed to even compete with a messaging campaign that moves at the speed of the Gutenberg Bible.

The U.S. needs to streamline any government programs and/or departments that are actively countering the IS message, making sure that the counter-narrative is a steadfast projection of the strategic and military failures of the Islamic State as well as its waning establishment of a caliphate.

THE ROLE OF THE MAINSTREAM MEDIA

The responsibility for counter-narratives is not just that of the government, but also that of the mainstream media outlets who draw in audiences by dwelling in the horrific and gruesome news, whether terrorism or upticks in domestic homicide. While the government does not need to be the face of all IS counter-narratives, it should take the lead in framing the message for media outlets and community organizations to adapt from. Often the government is an entity that is being vilified in jihadist messages, so the risk of basing all counter-branding to potential IS recruits in the U.S. or Western governments could de-legitimize the message. The importance of simultaneously fighting a digital battle to quell the spread of IS ideology has been understated until quite recently, but is as crucial as the military front. As Bertram (2016, Pg. 225) notes, "A digital problem needs a digital solution", and that is precisely what the international community has on its hands with the Islamic State. The hearts and minds of the youth are at stake and so is the advancement of caliphate utopianism as well as jihadi worship among disaffected global youth.

As Koehler (2014, Pg. 118) states, "The internet provides a perceived constraint-free space and anonymity. This provokes or motivates individuals to speak or act out more radically online as they would normally do offline." The virtual caliphate that IS has constructed allows for supporters from the Middle East region and around the world to participate and assist the group in furthering their mission, while feeling little pressure from law enforcement or corporations to disengage on their platforms.

Counter-narratives do not necessarily need to be constructs of the government, and often occur in an organic fashion, with members of a conversation thread or a particular network tapping into combat jihadist messages. This response promulgated largely by the digital activist community and non-governmental organizations, such as the Institute for Strategic Dialogue could be the most effective response to extremist ideology online. The Islamic State has been methodical in its co-option of Western culture, hashtags that are of interest to Western audiences, and pervasive presence on Western-dominated social media platforms and websites, which has created a culture of "jihobbyists" (Brachman, 2008, Pg. 19). Terror organizations like IS understand that a majority of those who consume their message online will never travel to the Middle East or become devout practitioners of Sharia, but will package the propaganda in order to reach the specified Western audience who promulgates the message, whether for shock value or in support, to their network and beyond. Governments, corporations, and the international community (including non-governmental, private sector, and activist groups) have a vested interest in coordinating to fight the spread of IS and extremist ideology, as more lone wolf actors are attacking soft targets and civilian casualties are the main goal.

BIG DATA AND COUNTERTERRORISM

The existence of big data, or large sets of data points that can be captured, aggregated, stored, and analyzed is a side effect of the global digital society, and can be used to predict revolutionary patterns, examine mobilization stimuli in social movements, as well as to build a network of terrorist connections in order to destabilize a jihadist organization. Governments around the world have taken to collecting massive pools of data from citizens and foreigners alike in order to prevent the next attack. Couch and Robins (2013, Pg. 10) note,

...In the field of cyber-security...Big Data analytics are being applied to spot advanced persistent threats – such as socially engineered attacks designed to steal corporate intellectual property or government information.

Big data is being applied by international organizations such as NATO's Allied Rapid Reaction Corps HQ, which works with the academic sector to develop methods for utilizing Big Data in open-source intelligence to predict vulnerable targets for radicalization, individuals as well as communities (Couch & Robbins, 2013). The intelligence communities are realizing that using analytics in place of humans can speed the process of analyzing and preventing radicalization or attacks, and thus incorporating digital methods in counterterrorism efforts. Chris Sailer noted,

The ability to [leverage Big Data analytics] is a combination of brute computing capacity and the ability to collect [data] at an astronomical scale. But the other part is leveraging advanced analytics and graph stories and cognitive computing platform to be able to do what a human analyst can't (Woodie, 2014).

The U.S. Department of Defense developed the Minerva initiative that seeks to identify social unrest and insurgencies at a domestic level as well as abroad. According to Woodie (2014), the program uses data mining to analyze and determine threats using data points acquired from Twitter and other digital sources. In addition, as suggested in this work, the public sector is being consulted with marginally (but could be used in a more effective manner by governments), for example, the Washington D.C.-based company GIS Federal is consulting with the U.S. Cyber Center of Excellence to monitor terrorist movements in Syria and Iraq using the a database that received information and data from drones and is "able to plot the data across space and time" (Woodie, 2014). This gives the U.S. military the ability to analyze geographic data with other sources to provide a larger picture of what a terrorist or organization may be planning.

The U.S. National Security Agency (NSA) has been collecting Big Data since the enactment of the Patriot Act to identify potential threats to the U.S., and the data collected ranges from phone metadata to information pulled from social media, which has caused uncertainty regarding the role of the agency, and the civil liberties of American citizens. NSA Director and commander of the U.S. Cyber Command, Mike Rogers underscored the concerns in a February 2015 speech, stating

The metadata collection generates value for the nation. I honestly believe that. Is it a silver bullet that in and of itself guarantees that there will never be another 9/11 or there won't be a successful terrorist attack? My comment would be 'No'...It is one component of a broader strategy designed to help enhance our security (Tadjdeh, 2015).

The use of Big Data in counterterrorism is in a developmental phase, as governments, the private sector, and individual citizens around the world are grappling with how much information is necessary to thwart potential attacks without unraveling civil rights and liberties in democratic countries. As Professor Bhavani Thuraisingham notes, "While Big Data can help in predicting or analyzing terrorist attacks, government agencies and companies employing the technology must be mindful of privacy concerns" (Tadjdeh, 2015).

The next chapter addresses the issue of bureaucracy in Western governments, particularly the United States that disallows or discourages non-governmental assistance in the fight against IS, but the hacker and activist community around the world have shown a great interest in liberating, at very least, the digital space from the dishonest and detrimental messaging of the Islamic State. The Islamic State presents a precarious challenge for an already strained international community, for reasons highlighted throughout the work, including BREXIT, a turn toward nationalism and away from globalism, and the strategic issues of coordinating counterterrorism efforts among nations who are wary of each other as well as their common enemy (i.e.: Russia and the United States conducting simultaneous airstrikes in Syria). Governments around the world are facing citizenries that are less trusting and want more local control, favoring a focus on domestic issues and successes over a transnational, regional, or international cooperative. At a moment when citizens are most uncertain about their state institutions and politics, they must rely on those same institutions to combat the threat of IS and other extremist ideologies, both physically and digitally. The governments have yet to step completely into the role of digital combatant and have little authority or appetite to hold corporations accountable for content disseminated on their social media platforms. Western governments in particular are in a sticky situation, attempting to provide for civil liberties such as freedom of expression and speech while being able to conduct the type of surveillance that can save lives and thwart attacks.

REFERENCES

Apps, P. (2015, Dec. 29). Major poll says 74% of Britons expect a major terrorist attack in 2016. *The Independent.* Retrieved from http://www.independent.co.uk/news/uk/home-news/2016-predictions-polled-britons-say-donald-trump-will-disappear-from-us-politics-and-uk-will-suffer-a6789686.html

Berger, J. M. (2015, March 6). *The ISIS Twitter census: Making sense of ISIS's use of Twitter*. Brookings Institute. Retrieved from https://www.brookings.edu/blog/order-from-chaos/2015/03/06/the-isis-twitter-census-making-sense-of-isiss-use-of-twitter/

Berger, J. M., & Strathearn, B. (2013). Who Matters Online: Measuring Influence, Evaluating Content and Countering Violent Extremism in Online Social Networks. *Developments in Radicalization and Political Violence.* International Centre for the Study of Radicalization and Political Violence. Retrieved from http://icsr.info/wp-content/uploads/2013/03/ICSR_Berger-and-Strathearn.pdf

Bertram, L. (2016). Terrorism, the Internet and the Social Media Advantage: Exploring how terrorist organizations exploit aspects of the internet, social media and how these same platforms could be used to counter-violent extremism. *Journal for Deradicalization,* (7), 225-252.

Bill C-51. (2015). *Canadian Legislation*. Retrieved from https://openparliament.ca/bills/41-2/C-51/

Brachman, J. (2008). *Global Jihadism: Theory and Practice*. New York: Routledge.

Brooking, E., & Singer, P. W. (2016, Nov.). War goes Viral. *The Atlantic.* Retrieved from http://www.theatlantic.com/magazinc/archivc/2016/11/war-goes-viral/501125/

Browne, R., & Starr, P. (2016, June 20). CIA director grave warning: ISIS dangerous as ever. *CNN.* Retrieved from http://www.cnn.com/2016/06/16/politics/john-brennan-cia-isis/

Couch, N., & Robins, B. (2013). *Big Data for Defence and Security*. Occasional Paper, Royal United Services Institute. Retrieved from https://www.ndm.net/datawarehouse/pdf/big-data-for-defence-and-security-report-final.pdf

Drennen, J. (2014). Who has Contributed What in the Coalition Against the Islamic State? *Foreign Policy.* Retrieved from http://foreignpolicy.com/2014/11/12/who-has-contributed-what-in-the-coalition-against-the-islamic-state/

Gartenstein-Ross, D. (2015, Jan. 6). The Decline of ISIS Has Already Begun. *The Atlantic.* Retrieved from http://www.theatlantic.com/international/archive/2015/01/the-decline-of-isis-syria-iraq/384261/

Glavin, N. (2015, Dec. 7). Counter ISIS' Narratives on Social Media. *The New York Times.* Retrieved from http://www.nytimes.com/roomfordebate/2015/12/06/how-can-america-counter-the-appeal-of-isis/counter-isis-narratives-on-social-media

Hong, N. (2016, Aug. 28). U.S. Revamps Line of Attack in Social-Media Fight Against Islamic State. *Wall Street Journal.* Retrieved from http://www.wsj.com/articles/u-s-revamps-line-of-attack-in-social-media-fight-against-islamic-state-1472415600

Ignatius, D. (2014, Sept. 18). James Clapper: We underestimated the Islamic State's 'will to fight'. *The Washington Post.* Retrieved from https://www.washingtonpost.com/opinions/david-ignatius-we-underestimated-the-islamic-state-james-clapper-says/2014/09/18/f0f17072-3f6f-11e4-9587-5dafd96295f0_story.html?utm_term=.a77014d7cc07

Karatzogianni, A. (2015, Nov. 18). Anonymous hackers could be Islamic State's online nemesis. *The Conversation.* Retrieved from http://theconversation.com/anonymous-hackers-could-be-islamic-states-online-nemesis-50876

Kholmann, E. (2005, Aug. 2). Al Qaeda and the Internet. *Washington Post.* Retrieved from http://www.washingtonpost.com/wp-dyn/content/discussion/2005/08/05/DI2005080501262.html

Kirk, A. (2016, March 24). Iraq and Syria: How many foreign fighters are fighting for Isil. *The Telegraph.* Retrieved from http://www.telegraph.co.uk/news/2016/03/29/iraq-and-syria-how-many-foreign-fighters-are-fighting-for-isil/

Koehler, D. (2014). The Radical Online: Individual Radicalization Processes and the Role of the Internet. *Journal for Deradicalization.* (1). Retrieved from http://journals.sfu.ca/jd/index.php/jd/article/view/8/8

Mastracci, D. (2015, March 2). Islamophobia sells in Canada. *Al Jazeera America.* Retrieved from http://america.aljazeera.com/opinions/2015/3/islamophobia-sells-in-canada.html

Miller, G., & Higham, S. (2015, May 8). In a propaganda war against ISIS, the U.S. tried to play by the enemy's rules. *Washington Post.* Retrieved from https://www.washingtonpost.com/world/national-security/in-a-propaganda-war-us-tried-to-play-by-the-enemys-rules/2015/05/08/6eb6b732-e52f-11e4-81ea-0649268f729e_story.html

Navarro, J., & Villaverde, J. (2014). The future of counter-terrorism in Europe. The need to be lost in the correct direction. *European Journal of Future Research, 2*(50).

Reuters. (2016, July 20). *100 jihadis still entering Syria from Turkey each week.* Retrieved from http://www.reuters.com/article/us-mideast-crisis-syria-idUSKCN1000VU

Strategic Implementation Plan for Empowering Local Partners to Prevent Violent Extremism in the United States. (2011, Dec). Executive Office of the President of the United States. Retrieved from https://www.whitehouse.gov/sites/default/files/sip-final.pdf

Tadjdeh, Y. (2015, April). *Big Data Helping to Pinpoint Terrorist Activities, Attacks.* Retrieved from http://www.nationaldefensemagazine.org/archive/2015/April/Pages/BigDataHelpingtoPinpointTerroristActivitiesAttacks.aspx

Talbot, D. (2015, Sept. 30). Fighting ISIS Online. *MIT Technology Review.* Retrieved from https://www.technologyreview.com/s/541801/fighting-isis-online/

The Daily Express. (2016, Dec. 9). *More than half of Germans see refugees as country's biggest problem.* Retrieved from http://www.express.co.uk/news/world/741822/Germany-Merkel-migrant-crisis-refugees-integration-biggest-problem

The Economist. (2016, April 18). *Israel is using social media to prevent terrorist attacks.* Retrieved from http://www.economist.com/news/middle-east-and-africa/21697083-new-paradigm-intelligence-israel-using-social-media-prevent-terrorist

Travis, A. (2016, Aug. 24). MPs say Facebook, Twitter and YouTube 'consciously failing' to tackle extremism. *The Guardian.* Retrieved from https://www.theguardian.com/politics/2016/aug/25/mps-facebook-twitter-youtube-extremism-isis

Tufecki, Z. (2016, May 19). The Real Bias Built In at Facebook. *The New York Times.* Retrieved from http://www.nytimes.com/2016/05/19/opinion/the-real-bias-built-in-at-facebook.html

United Nations Security Council. (2014). Resolution 2178. Retrieved from http://www.un.org/en/sc/ctc/docs/2015/SCR%202178_2014_EN.pdf

Vitale, H. M., & Keagle, J. M. (2014). A time to tweet, as well as a time to kill: ISIS's projection of power in Iraq and Syria. *Defense Horizons,* (77). Retrieved from http://search.proquest.com/docview/1618549256?accountid=8289

Woodie, A. (2014, Oct. 14). *How Big Data Analytics Can Help Fight ISIS.* Retrieved from https://www.datanami.com/2014/10/14/big-data-analytics-can-help-fight-isis/

Chapter 4
The Role of the (H)Ac(k)tivist

INTRODUCTION

The previous chapter illuminated the necessity of Western governments to coordinate with one another in order combat the spread and strengthening of global jihadism. Yet there is also an underlying need to involve community, religious (most importantly, Muslim groups), and other civil society organizations that are not connected to the government formally, but are carrying the torch for the government through dialogue with potential recruits and disseminators of Islamic State ideology, particularly online. However, there remains many ethical questions about the tactics that some non-governmental organizations are using to combat extremism in social networks, namely that of the hacktivist community. While groups like Anonymous and GhostSec are working to dismantle the Islamic State's ability to fluidly recruit and communicate on their relied upon networks, their tactics are not endorsed by the governments in most Western countries, are typically illegal. Governments

DOI: 10.4018/978-1-5225-2190-7.ch004

like the United States have targeted hacker groups, such as Anonymous and their members for their disregard for cyber law as well as for their unorthodox tactics that range from trolling political officials and corporations, to distributed denial of service attacks (DDoS) that shut down website accessibility with a push of a button. So, although hacktivist groups are on the side of internet freedom, which happens to coincide with the governments' desire to remove IS ideology from social media and the internet entirely, what role should the non-governmental sector play in fighting an international digital war?

THE MAKING OF ANONYMOUS

Anonymous has been the most visible hacker organization on the scene in the last decade in the West. The group is a digital vigilante collective that are loosely organized around principles of internet freedom, non-censorship, and more recently, sociopolitical and justice issues that have caused a splinter among original members who were just around for the 'lulz,' or the laughs. Anonymous is a faceless entity that prides itself on being a single voice on whatever issue they may be tackling at the moment, which makes for an incredibly dangerous force if they are not acting for the common good. Anonymous became a collective through the online bulletin board, 4Chan, which is known for its controversial tactics to embarrass, disrupt, or dismantle an opponent through predominately digital means. The group began as a pseudo-'Dennis the Menace' style hackers who were interested in preserving internet freedom and used recreational hacking to disrupt networks or organizations that did not adhere to their standard. But throughout their evolution, the Anon members have developed a penchant for political justice, involving themselves in the global Occupy movements, Arab Spring, various rape cases in the West that did not provide adequate justice for the victims, and most recently, have declared cyber war on the Islamic State. The group uses an anonymous democratic voting system to choose their targets and flood social networks, websites and message boards with their ideology and beliefs, in hopes of furthering a political goal or social justice reform (Coleman, 2011).

Anonymous' actions are often counterintuitive and involve the varied skill sets of its members. They are often fighting for free speech and non-censorship of online spaces by shutting down websites, or spreading false information in order to ruin a target's life, business, and/or credibility. The group lives outside of the law in use of hacking techniques and compromising personal information of targets, making Anonymous a formidable foe that PayPal, the Church of Scientology, MasterCard, and many governments worldwide have had the pleasure of being tormented by. Hacking is implicitly political and makes a statement about how we [the consumer] should treat information, and Anonymous values information and knowledge above all.

The group operates as a modern day Platonic-society, shining information on the masses doomed to live in the allegorical cave of darkness. It is through the acquisition of truth via Anonymous' good deeds that the people are able to make their own value judgments as to how that truth affects their lives. The operational goals of Anonymous are reiterated on their website noting, "We must all speak out against the obliteration of our privacy by governments everywhere and to stop the persecution of activists by vindictive governments" (AnonOps, 2015). By 2011, Anonymous was operational in in Italy, Venezuela, Brazil, Syria, Bahrain, Tunisia, Egypt and Libya (Coleman, 2011), which shows the reach of the Anon brand. As well as being operational in Syria before the Islamic State, which provides a strategic cyber advantage that Western governments are not as lucky to have. The sentiment of speaking for those who cannot speak for themselves would soon extend to non-state actors such as the victims of the Islamic State, and the purview of Anonymous actions would move beyond fighting for stratified causes but a mass collective of individuals with varied technological skills attempting to disrupt messaging that it has deemed dangerous to a populace and disseminating truth. Karatzogianni (2015) explains that

Anonymous takes the position that it is fighting against those who coordinate or commit crimes against humanity....its ideology therefore seeks to be inclusive and reflect a common humanity, which embraces, open, fluid identities that are not restricted to nationality, religion or ethnicity.

ANONYMOUS 'JOINS UP'

Before engaging in cyber war with the Islamic State, Anonymous redefined itself as less a prankster organization as in the days of attacking Scientology, and identifying with the struggle of citizen actors worldwide who lived under authoritarian regimes or governments that were not forthcoming by Anon standards (including the United States at times). It is worth noting that Anonymous was a crucial part of supporting the Arab Spring movements in

Tunisia and Egypt particularly through hashtag activism. The group launched #OpTunisia in January 2011 and mobilized to dismantle seven of the Tunisian government's official websites, including the Ministry of Industry and stock exchange (BBC, 2011). The group's revolutionary actions did not end in Tunisia but followed the Arab Spring trajectory, next assisting Egyptian citizens during the 25 January movement after President Hosni Mubarak shut off internet connectivity to the nation. Anonymous launched #OpEgypt and instructed citizens on how to get back online using the dark net as well as third party proxies.

Most importantly to this work, Anonymous provided hacking instructions and secure drop boxes during the build-up of the Syrian conflict that turned civil war, where protestors were able to deposit information and content anonymously (Coleman, 2011). The political operations of the organization tend to come together in a random manner and without forethought, which makes it a particularly dangerous enemy because their capabilities are known but their target is often only made aware of their sin once Anonymous has attacked.

On November 15, 2015, just two days after the attack on the Bataclan and throughout Paris that killed 130 and injured an estimated 350 people, Anonymous declared war on the Islamic State, who claimed responsibility for the attack (NYT, 2015). In less than a week, Anonymous reportedly took down 20,000 IS-related Twitter accounts, and clearly highlighted the unwillingness or lack of resources (including adequate staff) within corporations to devote toward counterterrorism efforts. While seemingly a good thing that the Islamic State's message is being actively combated by Anonymous and other groups, should it be the role of non-governmental organizations, and even more pointedly a hacktivist group, to remove content single-handedly, thus limiting free speech?

CONFLICT OF INTEREST?: USING NON-STATE ACTORS TO ELIMINATE A CYBER THREAT

The declaration of cyber war made by anonymous against the Islamic State communication apparatus is illustrative of the shifting dynamics of international conflict in the digital age. Analyzing the situation from a foreign policy lens, the war is between two non-state actors and the rules of engagement are nil. Michael Steinbach, head of the Federal Bureau of Investigation's counterterrorism division argues that Anonymous' declaration of war on IS qualifies as counterterrorism, and notes that the actions of hacker groups are perceived as vigilante tactics that undermine the rule of law and international standards of justice. Steinbach's statements confound and highlight the contradictory nature of allowing non-state activists to engage in efforts that have traditionally been left to government and military establishments.

There are strategic advantages to allowing, encouraging, and possibly enabling Anonymous and other like-minded hacktivist groups in pursuing counterterrorism efforts through non-governmental means (which would require ethical reflexivity on the part of the state). Membership of both the Islamic State and Anonymous remains young, technologically savvy, and are convinced of the potential in digital and social media tools. Anonymous adapted itself from a solely online collective of individuals to a social justice movement in the public sphere; whereas IS established itself physically first, and has used the internet and social media to garner international attention, and certainly for recruitment. One thing that is identical about the group is their constant presence online, in social networks and on communication platforms. This sustained digital presence provides an opportunity for the United States to utilize the actions of Anonymous to their benefit.

Steinbach noted in 2015 that the amount of jihadist, and particularly, Islamic State propaganda that is posted daily is a "full time job" and a "challenge to monitor" (Brown & Bruer, 2015). This means that the counterterrorism bureaucracy that is in effect currently in the United States is woefully inept and unable to keep up with the copious amounts of content that are unleashed via digital means daily. As Karatzogianni notes (2015), "In some respects, Anonymous is the perfect online vigilante nemesis to IS because of the failure of established states to organize any effective counter." This author would encourage the coordination of public-private partnerships to provide for a more inclusive, effective means of disrupting Islamic State communication. The involvement of the Muslim community in Western nations, in the mind of this author, becomes the lynchpin to combating lone-wolf terrorism on the ground. In terms of hacktivists, Anonymous exists to dismantle whatever their latest target is, so they have another strategic advantage on the counterterrorism bureaucracy: time. Anonymous has the time to devote to an all-day, full-time job of dispelling, deleting, and providing counter narratives to Islamic State ideology, where staffing enough government officials to devote the same energy to IS propaganda would be costly and as discussed in Chapter 3, may be ineffective regardless due to the messaging Western governments have spread thus far.

Where governments must adhere to domestic and international law, norms, and standards when conducting digital war, the flexible and non-hierarchical nature of Anonymous allows for a more robust, swift attack of Islamic State propaganda and digital infrastructure. For example, the open-source Low Orbit Ion Cannon (LOIC) that Anonymous developed for use by any Anon allows the member to volunteer their bandwidth to DDoS with a simple push of a button. While it may seem like a minor disruption, the LOIC has been used to dismantle heavily protected government websites (including that of the Egyptian government). The LOIC allows for members without any hacking or technological skills to simply download the tool, follow basic instructions to route the IP address, and overload the site instantaneously.

The Islamic State and Anonymous have one crucial similarity, their love of Twitter as a tool of both communication and as one of disruption. For example, in June 2016 Anonymous member known as Wauchula Ghost, hacked into hundreds of Islamic State sympathizers' Twitter accounts and posted pornography to taunt orthodox members (Bogage, 2016). This was in response to the Orlando club shooting, which Federal Bureau of Investigations (FBI) Director James Comey stated is "highly confident [the perpetrator] was radicalized at least in some part through the internet" (Bogage, 2016). The replacement of IS images and ideology with pornographic images is certainly not the optimal solution, but as a disruption of relied upon networks, it does aid in deterring recruitment, if even for a few hours. Members of the hacktivist community who have received media attention have displayed a relentless need to remove jihadist content from public spaces online, though using illegal means is a method of counterterrorism that Western nations would be smart to use advantageously. Dangerous precedents are set in times of war constantly, arming rebel factions in Syria, for example. The most short-sighted decision that the United States in particular could make in counterterrorism is not looking to the hacker community for, at the very least, tricks and tools for fighting a 21st century digital war.

Greg Housh has been associated with the Anonymous organization since its inception and noted that

Everyone loves to say 'hacking,' but what Anonymous is doing is just tons of research, identifying and monitoring everything out there that ISIS might

use to communicate and recruit, and trying to get those channels shut down, be it Twitter accounts, Facebook pages, telegram channels (Borchers, 2015).

This is the same mission that Western governments who are attempting to combat the jihadist ideology that has permeated the internet over the last three years, and have yet to make a considerable mark on the terrorist organization's online presence. Following the November 2015 attacks in Paris, Anonymous released instructional guides for DDoS attacks, how to decode passwords, how to create programs that identify IS-related accounts on Twitter, and how to assist the group in locating terrorist-propaganda hot spot online (Young, 2015).

GHOSTSEC

Ghost Security Group or GhostSec have joined Anonymous in their quest to rid the internet of IS ideology, taking down a website associated with the group on the dark web, and "replaced calls for jihad against the infidels with an advertisement for an online pharmacy peddling Prozac and Viagra" (Young, 2015). GhostSec is a collective of self-proclaimed former military officials working with computer security professionals who broke away from Anonymous proper due to a difference in tactics. GhostSec takes a more cautious approach to the censorship of content than Anonymous, who have in the quest to rid the internet of IS messaging and content, have taken down innocent Muslim websites (Schatz, 2015). Ghost Security Group differs from the Anonymous creed in one other major way: they cooperate with government officials as to not disturb ongoing counterterrorism efforts. Schatz (2015) reports directly following the November Paris attacks, Ghost Security members began "collecting Telegram channels and identifying social media accounts and sending them to U.S. authorities" and have claimed to have taken down 149 IS-associated sites and over social media accounts since January.

Naim (2014) notes the rise of "government-organized non-governmental organizations" (GONGO), or the increasing trend of the government recruiting sectors of the civil society to conduct traditionally government business. Naim focuses on the use of civilians to fight government wars in Syria for example, but the concept could be applied to counterterrorism as well. Civilian corps of hackers, private sector technology experts working in coordination with the government as well as community groups, such as religious organizations would provide a crucial blow to the 'hearts and minds' part of the war on IS, which is a critical part of quelling the spread of the ideology in the future.

FBI Director Comey stated on September 27, 2016 at a hearing before the Senate Homeland Security and Governmental Affairs Committee that the destruction of the Islamic State caliphate in Iraq and Syria will produce a "terrorist diaspora in the next two to five years like we have never seen before" (Shinkman, 2016). Comey points to the military destruction of the physical caliphate, which will likely push IS foreign fighters back to their nations of origin to promulgate violence in the name of the jihadist movement. This includes Western Europe and the United States, meaning that if these governments do not gain control of the ideological battle being conducted online, the foreign fighters returning home may have a more willing group of participants. The facilitation of dialogue between governments and civil society (including private sector technologists, the hacker community, and social/religious organizations) will be a critical part of the solution to a more comprehensive defeat of the Islamic State. As this chapter began, a military assault is not going to be enough this time, not to defeat an ideology. As Hanson (2015) notes,

A network can be difficult enough to combat, but a regionally organized grouping presents even greater challenges national terror ...yet the appeal of ISIS across the region coupled with new technology to connect extremists is laying the groundwork for this very network (Pg. 3).

The question of bureaucracy comes into play when discussing a valid, effective partnership between the decentralized and unruly Anonymous organization and the orderly establishment of the State. Weinstein (2015) argues that the U.S. government's digital battle against the Islamic State has been overly complicated by the bureaucracy and offers too few details and results. Rick Stengel supervises the Center for Strategic Counterterrorism Communications concluded that the CSCC is morphing into something called the Global Engagement Center,

which is to help optimize these kinds of third-party messages and help optimize these groups and do some seed funding with those groups and help them figure out how to message against this pernicious message that's out there (Miller & Higham, 2015).

This is an important point that must be recognized by more bureaucratic entities in order for effective communication from the societal level to potential recruits. The Global Engagement Center (GEC) was established in March 2016 via an executive order signed by President Obama, the center is focused on

coordinating whole-of-government efforts to discredit IS ideology

and seeks to

cultivate and support a global network of partners – governments, NGOs, and other organizations – who can serve as credible messengers against ISIS and provide positive alternative (New America, 2016).

'JAMMING' AND CULTURAL APPROPRIATION FROM THE CONSUMER SIDE

A tactic that Anonymous and other hacktivist organizations are taking advantage is described by Cammaerts (2007, Pg. 71) as "political jamming" - an attempt to change the behavior, thoughts and beliefs of content consumers by using memes and other visual content to market political messaging, whether positive or negative. The content must be amusing and engage the correct audience for the content to go viral, reaching mainstream recognition. For example, in September 2016, the Anti-Defamation League declared 'Pepe the Frog' a racist image, yet the image remains widely circulated by supporters of Donald Trump for President (Mele, 2016). The frog meme has featured swastikas and anti-Semitic content, and has spread from internet forums such as 4chan and Reddit to the mainstream via social media, and has come to symbolize the vitriol that characterizes the 2016 presidential election in the U.S.

The government must understand the importance of capturing the attention of the target audience, which is between the ages of 18-29 who are most likely to be swayed by IS propaganda. Political jamming would be an effective means to counter IS content by both the government as well as the civil society. A partnership would be required, as the government would need the social media networks, religious communities, and average citizens to promulgate an inclusive, positive message, (or simply one that mocks the strength that IS projects). A strategy of political jamming would allow the civil society to customize their messages to counter the Islamic State propaganda and provide diversified content to reach a multitude of target audiences. This would also support the notion that the community and citizenry in Western nations may be more effective at marketing content toward their own people/neighborhoods than the government, which can often muddle the message or create content that seems inauthentic or preachy.

ISIS-chan (Figure 1) is an example of political jamming at its finest. After the abduction of Japanese citizens by the Islamic State, Japanese animators created ISIS-chan, an anime character in all black garb who mocks the IS mission and existence. According to an ISIS-wiki page, ISIS-chan is a counterterrorism movement on the internet "by disturbing their search engine optimization (SEO) profile of related keywords with images of a cute character." ISIS-chan is particularly memorable when portrayed not as an innocently drawn schoolgirl but as a provocative, sexy character that is completely offensive to the Islamic State supporters and their ideology. Anime culture can be used as a tool of political/cultural jamming as a mechanism to populate social networks that are normally dominated by IS propaganda with content that counters the narrative as well as engages the audience.

Content such as ISIS-chan as well as using popular culture symbols can be useful anti-jihadist messages because they are "packaged, delivered and digested for wider audiences…we are all prodded and driven by narratives – by stories, images, slogans, memes, and stereotypes," states former CSCC

Figure 1. ISIS-chan; Photo from CNN Money, 2015

head Alberto Fernandez (Weinstein, 2015). This sort of cultural content that is used in a political manner can also provide a glimpse into the values of those spreading the message, humanizing IS targets and victims as well as providing a legitimate voice to Western governments by using memes and popular content to spread messages of equality and anti-extremist language through society in a decentralized fashion, not from the top-down. The risk of Western governments denigrating the IS message to the point of generalizing IS with all Muslims becomes a reality when the governments leave the development of the message to bureaucrats. The civil society, including religious organizations and hackers lend authenticity to anti-IS campaigns and counter-narratives, making it less likely that the digital campaign will be reduced to a clash of civilizations. As Weinstein (2015) notes,

If you're trying to sincerely engage young Muslim populations to dissuade them from supporting ISIS, your conversation needs to meet them on their level to be credible....To be able to articulate how murder and torture are un-Islamic, you have to be conversant in Islamic jurisprudence and cultures.

USING THE CIVIL SOCIETY AS A DE-RADICALIZING AGENT

Western governments are in imminent danger, according to FBI Director James Comey, of the impending diaspora of foreign fighters moving back to their homelands from Iraq and Syria. The necessity to pull the established Muslim communities closer to these governments in the U.S., France, Germany, the U.K., the Netherlands, etc. is more crucial than ever before. Facilitation of the Muslim civil society in social media networks may be the best deterrent for a young potential recruit to the Islamic State, by having their peers who understand their plight speaking directly to their pain, but also to their hope for a better life, one with inclusivity. Individual groups of activists such as Raqqa Is Being Slaughtered Silently (who host a Twitter account among other social media accounts) are making sure that their story from the ground in Syria is being heard across the world.

These accounts that host content directly from the Islamic State battlegrounds depicts the conditions that average citizens are having to endure when their government is fighting IS and rebel factions looking to replace the Assad regime where civilians are simply collateral damage, can be the most effective tool in stalling recruitment of Western citizens as IS foreign fighters (Weinstein, 2015). The digital campaign against the Islamic State may be perceived as a drop in the bucket compared to the military battle in Syria, Iraq, and now Libya. Yet, in terms of gaining control over the IS narrative that has saturated the internet, it behooves Western governments and counterterrorism agencies to assemble a collective of citizens, private sector businesses, and bureaucrats to provide ample counter messages.

Recruiting the civil society and facilitating self-identification/reporting of IS propaganda online as suggested by this author is becoming a reality overseas. In April 2016, U.K. officials launched a campaign to stop the spread of jihadist content online (Dodd, 2016). The campaign encourages citizens to report any IS content to authorities, and Helen Ball, the senior national coordinator for counterterrorism policing (U.K.) concludes, "The Counter Terrorism Internet Referral Unit has put considerable effort into prompting the removal of terrorist and extremist material. We know that communities are very concerned about this material – and communities defeat terrorism, which is why police and the public will continue to work together on this" (Dodd, 2016). This attitude needs to be implemented at a state level in the U.S. in order to more effectively identify IS content and flesh out potential recruits, or already engaged bad actors. There is a place for non-governmental organizations as well as individuals in the fight against the Islamic State in digital spaces, but it will take much more effort, time and resources than most governments have to offer to one goal. If one examines the fight against IS online in Anonymous terms, the internet is for all of us, an egalitarian tool that must be protected from perversion, and the Islamic State's vulgar propaganda and recruitment tactics have endangered the very spaces Anons fight to keep free.

The fight against the Islamic State's progression in both a physical and psychological sense are predicated on their ability to maintain legitimacy as a state and convince not just Muslims in the proximity to the caliphate itself, but also by having a sustained presence in the minds of global Muslims who may eventually come around to the group's way of thinking (or so IS hopes). According to US Department of the Air Force, "Terrorists act in the physical environment not to make tactical gains in the physical environment, but to wage strategic battle in the information environment" (Emery et al., 2005, Pg. 10). This is particularly true of the IS and their need to perpetuate their strength and military achievements in order to legitimize their caliphate. It is not enough in the digital age to simply wage jihad in the physical realm, but to be a lasting organization in a 24/7 news cycle, an organization must be able to control the information, content, and narrative online.

The Islamic State is undoubtedly winning this part of the battle because they are equipped with more than enough tech savvy recruits on the ground in Iraq and Syria, but also because they have effectively created a market for consumption of the content produced by the group. One can see the reach of the Islamic State each time a new beheading video is released, it takes often moments for the video to reach the mainstream media, and go viral on social media thanks to the multitude of supporters, sympathizers, and those who are dangerously ignorant of what the consequences of spreading IS propaganda are. Marks et al. (2010, Pg. 86) assert that the ""propagandistic effect" is the single greatest weapon available to "the revolutionaries in their position of asymmetry." This ensures that the group's ideology, tactics, tools and tricks will live forever in the cyber realm, even if the terrorist organization eventually splinters or dissolves completely.

This author argues that the most effective manner in which to fight digital jihad is by instituting public-private task forces and alliances among local communities and the government that encourage the reporting of suspicious online content, language or activity that is related to the Islamic State. Adams (2016) argues, "A more balanced approach between use of force and alternative or unorthodox counterterrorism methods will become necessary and a more influential aspect of many nation-state security postures as the fifth domain continues to be exploited by extremist groups." By controlling the information spaces through use of both bureaucratic and civil society resources, including the social media corporations that are so far not being held liable for the spreading of extremist content on their platforms, Western governments can greatly increase their ability to combat the recruitment of supporters on the ground, reducing the potential for lone wolf attacks as well as coordinated attacks if the diaspora that James Comey predicts come to fruition.

The hacker community has invaluable experience, tools, and resources that governments, particularly the United States could benefit from in their digital campaign to eliminate the Islamic State. Modern warfare involves nation-states battling non-state actors, as the world is witnessing in Syria for example. The tactics of fighting a non-state regime are often excessive when speaking militarily, and have put millions of civilians in the region at risk of death or being displaced. So utilizing a sector of Western society who can effectively battle a digital demon under the guidance of bureaucratic entities does not seem completely out of the realm of good judgment, particularly if the means justify the ends, and most would argue in the case of slowing the Islamic State's recruitment and ideological gains in the West, the means certainly justify the ends. As Cornish et al. (2010, Pg. 10) note, "In cyber warfare, the boundaries are blurred between the military and the civilian, the physical and the virtual, and power can be exerted by states or non-state actors, or by proxy."

The necessity of Western governments to act alone in combatting particularly digital enemies is questionable in the modern age of warfare that includes elements of civil society, namely social media and communication platforms to spread jihadist content. The content is not put up by state actors, so then why is it only the role of the government to monitor and remove content? The alliance between public actors and the various bureaucracies necessary to adequately patrol the internet and its various communicative platforms that has been suggested in this work must come with explicit instructions as to avoid censorship as well as issues of discrimination that have been reported in October 2016 in the U.K.'s PREVENT program. In October 2016, "The Science of Pre-Crime" report was released by CAGE and details academic and expert objections to the U.K. government's statutory requirement for public employees to identify signs of radicalization using a method developed by psychologists Christopher Dean and Monica Lloyd using "22 factors derived from a tool called Extremist Risk Guidance 22+" (CAGE, 2016). The CAGE spokesman, Ibrahim Mohamoud noted in 2015,

The PREVENT strategy has no peer-reviewed evidentiary basis showing a link between violence and ideology... The PREVENT policy has facilitated an atmosphere in which Muslims are incriminated within a pre-crime space for nothing more than holding opinions that run contrary to those taken by government. This increases the likelihood of disenfranchisement as opposed to countering it (Verkaik, 2015).

There must be clearly established guidelines and procedures for not only identifying extremist content versus opposition content that may run contrary to the government but is not a threat to the security of the nation. The U.K. PREVENT program has clearly come under fire from the civil society, namely human rights organizations for unduly targeting citizens who are not in danger of radicalization but due to the lax guidelines in the 22+ system has flagged them as a risk. This is certainly a risk when a threat has influence over a majority of a single demographic (whether religious, political, ethnic, racial, etc.). Anonymous has been accused of removing innocent Muslims' webpages, and certainly stereotyping comes to play in moments of international insecurity. But as an increasingly less global environment emerges, it does become important to not only insulate one's own nation but to make sure that a government does so in a humane manner, as to not inflame anti-Western sentiment. As previously stated, the Islamic State is a non-state actor, which means that terrorism is not necessarily becoming less global, simply the nation-state system that has encouraged international cooperation, particularly on issues of counterterrorism since the early 2000s.

Recommendations for Western governments for inclusion of the non-governmental sector in counterterrorism efforts include the formulation of peer-reviewed and scientifically approved methods for detecting the potential for radicalization; providing a standardized script for engaging in conversation with the potential recruit/consumer of jihadist content – governments and the civil society should collaborate on cues that both volunteers from the private sector along with bureaucrats can customize to the situation they are reacting to in real-time. Governments should take more seriously the actions of hacktivist organizations such as GhostSec and Anonymous when those actors are working for the public good, and adopt more tactics from these groups as they have been far more effective in removing extremist content than the government; and finally, utilizing popular culture to speak to the youth culture about the dangers of religious extremism in all forms (not just Muslim-oriented).

The non-governmental and civil society sector offers a multitude of resources, ideas, and nuance to counterterrorism efforts that bureaucracy often are not privy to, or are bound by legalities that make effective action impossible. It has become increasingly important for governments around the world who are seeking to counter the IS narrative in their nations to understand that a human, non-government aspect has to come into play, as most terrorism is targeted at a specific government or way of life that is objectionable to the organization. Yet the government is not the best facilitator of counter-IS conversations among potential recruits, it would seem that their peers, religious leaders, and contact with those who have successfully escaped IS would benefit the counterterrorism effort immensely.

REFERENCES

Adams, Z. (2016). Fighting the Islamic State in the Fifth Domain: Transnational Terrorism in the Indo-Pacific. *SIR Journal of International Relations.* Retrieved from http://www.sirjournal.org/research/fighting-the-islamic-state

BBC. (2011, Jan. 4). Anonymous activists target Tunisian government sites. *BBC News.* Retrieved from http://www.bbc.com/news/technology-12110892

Bogage, J. (2016, June 14). This hacker is fighting ISIS by spamming its Twitter accounts with porn. *Washington Post.* Retrieved from https://www.washingtonpost.com/news/the-switch/wp/2016/06/14/this-hacker-is-fighting-isis-by-spamming-its-twitter-accounts-with-porn/

Borchers, C. (2015, Nov. 28). How will 'Anonymous' wage war on the Islamic State? One of its own tells us. *The Washington Post.* Retrieved from https://www.washingtonpost.com/news/the-fix/wp/2015/11/28/how-will-anonymous-wage-war-on-the-islamic-state-one-of-its-own-tells-us/

Brown, P., & Bruer, W. (2015, Feb. 3). *FBI Official: ISIS is recruiting teens.* Retrieved from http://www.cnn.com/2015/02/03/politics/fbi-isis-counterterrorism-michael-steinbach/

CAGE. (2016, Sept. 29). *The 'science' of pre-crime: The secret 'radicalisation' study underpinning PREVENT.* Retrieved from http://cage.ngo/publication/the-science-of-pre-crime/

Cammaerts, B. (2007). Citizenship, the Public Sphere, and Media. In Reclaiming the Media: Communication Rights and Democratic Media Roles, (pp. 1-9). Intellect Books, University of Chicago Press.

Coleman, G. (2011). From the Lulz to Collective Action. *The New Everyday: A Media Commons Project, 6.*

Cornish, P., Livingstone, D., Clemente, D., & Yorke, C. (2010). *On cyber warfare: A Chatham House Report.* The Royal Institute of International Affairs.

Dodd, V. (2016, April 14). Counter-terrorism drive for public to report online Isis propaganda. *The Guardian.* Retrieved from https://www.theguardian.com/uk-news/2016/apr/15/police-launch-crackdown-on-isis-internet-extremism

Emery, N., Werchan, J., & Mowles, D., Jr. (2005). Fighting Terrorism and Insurgency: Shaping the Information Environment. *Military Review.* Retrieved from http://www.au.af.mil/au/awc/awcgate/milreview/emery.pdf

Hanson, F. (2015). *Countering ISIS in Southeast Asia: The case for an ICT offensive*. Perth USAsia Centre. Retrieved from http://perthusasia.edu.au/usac/assets/media/docs/publications/FINAL_F_Hanson_ISIS_ICT.pdf

Karatzogianni, A. (2015, Nov. 18). Anonymous hackers could be Islamic State's online nemesis. *The Conversation*. Retrieved from http://theconversation.com/anonymous-hackers-could-be-islamic-states-online-nemesis-50876

Marks, T. A., Gorka, L. S., & Sharp, R. (2010). *Getting the next war right: Beyond population-centric warfare*. Institute for National Strategic Studies.

Mele, C. (2016, Sept. 27). Pepe the Frog Meme Listed as a Hate Symbol. *The New York Times*. Retrieved from http://www.nytimes.com/2016/09/28/us/pepe-the-frog-is-listed-as-a-hate-symbol-by-the-anti-defamation-league.html

Miller, G., & Higham, S. (2015, May 8). In a propaganda war against ISIS, the U.S. tried to play by the enemy's rules. *Washington Post*. Retrieved from https://www.washingtonpost.com/world/national-security/in-a-propaganda-war-us-tried-to-play-by-the-enemys-rules/2015/05/08/6eb6b732-e52f-11e4-81ea-0649268f729e_story.html

Naim, M. (2014, June 19). The Rise of Militarized NGOs. *The Atlantic*. Retrieved from http://www.theatlantic.com/international/archive/2014/06/the-rise-of-militarized-ngos/373074/

New America. (n.d.). *Fighting ISIS in the Information Space*. Retrieved from https://www.newamerica.org/international-security/events/fighting-isis-information-space/

New York Times. (2015, November). *Attack in Paris*. Retrieved from http://www.nytimes.com/news-event/attacks-in-paris

Schatz, B. (2015, Nov. 24). Inside Anonymous' Messy Cyberwar Against ISIS. *Mother Jones*. Retrieved from http://www.motherjones.com/politics/2015/11/anonymous-hacking-isis-ghost-security

Shinkman, P. (2016, Sept. 27). Military Success Against ISIS Will Create 'Terrorist Diaspora,' James Comey Says. *U.S. News*. Retrieved from http://www.usnews.com/news/articles/2016-09-27/military-success-against-isis-will-create-terrorist-diaspora-james-comey-says

Steinbach, M. (2015, June 3). *Terrorism Gone Viral: The Attack in Garland, Texas and Beyond*. Federal Bureau of Investigations. Statement before the House Homeland Security Committee. Retrieved from https://www.fbi.gov/news/testimony/terrorism-gone-viral-the-attack-in-garland-texas-and-beyond

Verkaik, R. (2015, July 10). Government deradicalisation plan will brand Muslims with beards as terrorists, say academics. *The Independent*. Retrieved from http://www.independent.co.uk/news/uk/politics/government-deradicalisation-plan-will-brand-muslims-with-beards-as-terrorists-say-academics-10381796.html

Weinstein, A. (2015, March 12). Here's How the US Should Fight ISIS With Social Media. *Wired*. Retrieved from https://www.wired.com/2015/03/heres-us-fight-isis-social-media/

Young, A. (2015, Nov. 28). How Anonymous Fights ISIS: It's More about Research Than Hacking. *International Business Times*. Retrieved from http://www.ibtimes.com/how-anonymous-fights-isis-its-more-about-research-hacking-2202869

Chapter 5
End Game

INTRODUCTION

In August 2016, King Mohammed VI of Morocco spoke to his mixed religious society asking,

Is it conceivable that God, the Most Merciful, the Most Compassionate could order someone to blow up himself or kill innocent people....[these people perverting the word of the Quran] are actually lying to Allah and His Messenger (Haddadin, 2016).

The Moroccan King, who is believed to be a direct descendent of the Prophet Mohammad, joins a growing list of Islamic leaders in the MENA region to publicly denounce the violence perpetrated by IS in the name of religious sanctity, including King Abdullah II of Jordan as recently as September 25, 2016 (Haddadin, 2016). The Islamic State has foundational roots in Jordan with al-Zarqawi, one of the leaders being born in the country, and the nation becoming linked to terrorism that was exposed by a botched

DOI: 10.4018/978-1-5225-2190-7.ch005

prisoner exchange between a Jordanian fighter pilot and a Japanese reporter for a female suicide bomber jailed by Jordan and at least one other prisoner. The fighter pilot was burned to death by the Islamic State in January 2015, which triggered an intense and visceral reaction to the terror organization by the public and the government, with the Jordanian government ordering three consecutive days of airstrikes on IS.

The public renouncement of IS, the vision of the caliphate, and reiteration that the group wholly perverts Islamic principles as well as slaughters indiscriminately is a narrative that must be encouraged and repeated, not just in the Middle East but around the world. Counter narratives to the Islamic State's call to jihad in order to build their utopia that is spread by prominent Muslim leaders, ideologues, and the civil society will help to combat the number of young Muslims who will be unduly enamored by IS propaganda. U.S. Secretary of State John Kerry noted, "Arab nations play a critical role, the leading role in the effort to repudiate, once and for all, the dangerous and insulting distortion of Islam that IS propaganda attempts to spread around the world" (Szep, 2014). The 'end game' with the Islamic State is tricky to diagnose, and even more difficult to envision in the current political environment.

As many military and political officials have acknowledged, the conflict with the Islamic State is going to require more than a combat mission to dismantle the physical boundaries and legitimacy of the state. Yet, as this author has noted and Haddadin (2016) succinctly concludes,

The state is not clear about where it stands, what message it wants to convey, what efforts have been made to confront and remedy social division and extremism, and the role of media in rebutting the fanatic discourse to maintain moderation, if any, especially putting an end to extremism and hate speech toward the other,

as has been argued throughout this volume.

The indifference displayed and ineffective programs implemented by Western governments to combat internet-enabled terrorist content and conversation has arguably set the effort to "ultimately degrade and destroy IS" (Obama, 2014) back considerably. It is clear that Western governments have not learned a valuable lesson from the exceedingly long War on Terror: that you can flesh out and eliminate an enemy's headquarters, training camps, and hiding places but you cannot carpet bomb an ideology, religious fanaticism, or simply opposition to certain types of governance (including democracy or adherence to the policies of a Western-dominated global market economy).

The strategy of the Islamic State in using social media and content-sharing platforms for communication of beliefs, tactics, and eventually recruitment has decentralized IS membership, allowing the organization to take root in 18 countries spanning from the MENA region to Central Africa to Southeast Asia (National Counterterrorism Center, 2016). Clearly, there are correlations to local chapters of Al Qaeda in many of the areas where IS support has strengthened. Yet the fact that IS-inspired and/or directed attacks are beginning to occur in Afghanistan does display the influence of the group in disparate corners of the globe, not usually susceptible to outside ideologies. The risk of not combatting internet-enabled terrorism and the dissemination of propaganda that aids in recruitment and inspiration of lone wolf terrorism increases, particularly after the military conflict has been completed, and the Islamic State no longer occupies sovereign land. As Daniel Benjamin, who served as the State Department's counterterrorism coordinator under the Obama administration noted, "Eliminating the caliphate will be an achievement – but more than likely, it will be the end of the beginning rather than the beginning of the end" (Trofimov, 2016).

WHAT IS NEXT?

The Islamic State, as of October 2016 controls half of the territory it claimed as part of its caliphate in 2014; Iraqi supported by U.S. airstrikes have systematically retaken major cities such as Tikrit and Ramadi, and hope to regain control of Mosul by the end of 2016 (Jadallah, 2016). Not only have major territorial gains been made against IS in Iraq but also in Libya (as the U.S. began airstrikes in the coastal city of Sirte) and Syria (again, the U.S. supporting the Syrian Democratic Force are moving in on Raqqa, the capital of the caliphate). As FBI Director James Comey warned in October 2016 regarding the imminent diaspora of IS foreign fighters once located in Iraq and Syria, "through the fingers [that crush the caliphate] are going to come hundreds of very, very dangerous people...they will not all die on the battlefield in Syria and Iraq" (Gerstein & Scholtes, 2016).

The immediate risk for the U.S. and its European counterparts is the open communication with citizens around the world and availability for recruitment before the diaspora begins in earnest. Richard Barrett, who worked in counter-extremism in MI6 (U.K.) states,

There will a greater threat as ISIS continues to lose territory, as numbers [of fighters flowing back to Europe] will increase and security services will be even more hard-pressed, making an attack more likely to slip through the net. This will lead to greater public anger, more pressure on security services, and it will become a spiral (Jadallah, 2016).

In a March 2016 report, the European Union's counterterrorism coordinator underscores the return of foreign fighters, stating that there are "well-founded estimates that around 5,000 EU citizens have traveled to Syria and Iraq to join IS and other extremist groups" (Levitt, 2016).

The worst-case scenario for Western countries that will experience the diaspora as much as Middle Eastern nations, is for trained Islamic State fighters returning to London, Berlin, New York City, Beirut, and beyond to be received by small legions of supporters who are pre-mobilized for the cause. This scenario seems all too real in the digital age where jihad is much easier to spread via social media, the organization's communications teams, and when it exists undisrupted in the recesses of the dark web. As the world has witnessed over 2016, the Islamic State's sphere of influence is wide, and the spread of lone wolf and small cell terror attacks has increased. These actors are often, (particularly, the lone wolf attacks occurring in the West), self-radicalized via the internet and IS digital recruitment strategies.

According to *The New York Times* citing a report released by West Point in October 2016, Islamic State media output has slowed dramatically since the increase in coalition airstrikes and the offensive to push the group away from major strongholds, such as Raqqa and Mosul intensify. Milton, author of the West Point report noted during its peak, the Islamic State was releasing upwards of 700 pieces of content from official sources in August 2015, which has declined to under 200 in August 2016, after a year of constant airstrikes (Milton, 2016). The decline in the amount of content being released could be in relation to the projection of strength that IS has continued to display in order to recruit new members and foreign fighters. Yet because of military losses, the ability for the Islamic State to legitimately portray the caliphate as a stable, strong, and happy place to be has dwindled. However,

Experts caution that the Islamic State's ideology, which portrays Muslims in an apocalyptic contest with non-Muslims, is likely to continue to inspire terrorist acts long after the caliphate is gone (Sommerville, 2016).

As discussed throughout the text, lone wolf terrorism has characteristics that link digital jihadist content, self-radicalization, and mental health/personality issues, the person may or may not be a devout believer in the organization to which they have pledged allegiance. According to Jeffrey Simon, "In the old days the lone wolf was the loner. Now, as this individual apparently pledged allegiance to ISIS, they can feel they are carrying out the work or a particular group, even if they have never met with the leaders or members" (Chotiner, 2016). But often the person does have personal issues that often affect their mental state when engaging in extremist content leading to lone wolf action.

Foreign Policy has continued to argue that the Islamic State's use of lone wolf terrorism has been overshadowed by the infusion of trained cells in European nations, including France and Belgium, demonstrating a shift in tactics from the stratified toward more coordinated, hierarchical attacks (Levitt, 2016). While *Foreign Affairs* has dubbed IS's lone wolf terrorism strategy a "myth" (Gartenstein-Ross & Barr, 2016), based on the analysis that shows officials have misused the term 'lone wolf' in describing events that have later been linked to terror cells, not an individual actor. The Islamic State is visibly moving toward a strategy of maximum damage and casualties in regions of the world where small cells of its membership have infiltrated or perhaps radicalized in Western nations (Brussels, Nice). Yet the fact that the organization/leadership are involved directly in some of the larger methodical attacks does not negate the instances of lone wolf terrorism that are evident, mainly in the United States, a nation where it is much harder for small cells of IS members to enter and plot since the enactment and extension of the Patriot Act.

The threat of lone wolf and individual terrorist actions remains a reality as long as the Islamic State and other extremist organizations are able to permeate Western networks in order elicit an affective response from marginalized citizens who are not able or willing to make the pilgrimage to the caliphate, but want to be active participants in the jihad. To eschew the possibilities of effective IS propaganda and content in recruitment and/or radicalization of Westerners is as dangerous as an over response on the part of Western governments, resulting in a suspension of civil liberties for law-abiding Muslims who denounce the actions of IS. As unsatisfying as it is, the counterterrorism capabilities of Western governments, the moral, ethical, and legal ramifications, and the unprecedentedly savvy use of Western platforms and networks by terror organizations is unchartered territory. International governments, the civil society, and private sector must strike a difficult balance to both combat extremism in the digital realm (which manifests in the public sphere), and not deteriorate rights to privacy or the freedoms that citizens (including Muslims) enjoy in democratic nations.

This delicate balance can be established if the suggestion for an increased global public-private alliance to monitor and eliminate extremist content becomes a priority. The inclusion of private sector citizens, including hacktivists would show good faith on the part of governments around the world who have increased domestic surveillance in the name of national security. As well as inclusion of the Muslim community in counterterrorism dialogue and spreading religious justifications as to why the Islamic State and other extremist organizations do not represent the Islamic faith or the majority of its adherents. Arguably, the worst thing that governments seeking to destroy safe spaces for IS content online can do is to turn inward and not utilize the rich political and religious messaging that can be more effectively espoused by the civil society.

To summarize the recommendations for counterterrorism in the digital age are as follows:

1. International governments must acknowledge the necessity of cooperation on not only military efforts but also stealth coordination among digital intervention units and government-instituted programs to combat extremist internet content. Obviously, the internet is not a national instrument but one that is global and the propaganda disseminated by the Islamic State on mainstream platforms, such as Twitter as well as the dark web is open for public consumption in an egalitarian manner. This level of interconnectedness in the digital realm also requires an equal if not greater level of international coordination among government and civil society. The international coalition that President Obama discussed in September 2014 needs to be more visible in a physical but certainly in a digital sense.
2. The acknowledgment from governments around the world that counterterrorism efforts must be "glocalized" (Friedman, 2005), or handled both locally and globally must accompany the realization that Islamic State will not simply be defeated militarily. The diaspora that Comey warns of coming in the next few years is a real challenge for all governments, as these foreign fighters have come from all parts of the world, and thus, will likely return to the diverse list of nations from which they originate. While many Western nations turn inward, becoming more nationalist in policies and ideology, the enemies of democracy watch in

wait, seeing the lack of coordination as a vulnerability to be exploited. This nationalism also threatens the stability of domestic counterterrorism efforts that have in some cases (such as reported by CAGE) have alienated the Muslim community who could be the key to uncovering future cells or attacks.

3. Governments should adopt tools and tactics from the hacktivist community as well as foster coordination among those skilled hackers who are aiding the government in identifying jihadist content without a formal invitation. Again, inclusion of the civil society, but particularly the hacker society who are most concerned with issues of privacy, surveillance, and security would show good faith on behalf of governments around the world. The era of state versus non-state actors has allowed for the bending of formal rules of engagement in political conflict, which this author argues can benefit governments who recognize the opportunities provided through the often more skilled and resource-rich (time, passion, education) hacktivist society around the world.
4. There must be a more visibly present and constant renouncement of the Islamic State and its perversion of the faith by Muslim leaders, both in the Middle East and abroad. This provision also includes the recruitment of Muslims in civil society to fight jihadist dialogue with an intimate knowledge of the Quran, exposing IS actions as anti-Islam. It is crucial for Western governments to encourage Muslims within their societies to come forward and report suspicious activity in public and digital spaces. The more those governments paint the IS problem as a solely Muslim problem, that encouragement wanes.
5. Infusion of popular culture memes, content, and messages of equality from the government and civil society need to be emphasized. The 'Think Again' program in the U.S. and the PREVENT program in the U.K. highlight problems that can emerge when the civil society and average citizens are not involved in counterterrorism dialogue online. Trolling potential recruits, using similar imagery to counter as the IS uses to recruit, and providing tools for identification of jihadists that may endanger liberties of peaceful citizens does nothing to assist governments in eliminating pro-IS sentiment. The use of internationally recognized content, actors, and messages can effectively reach the most targeted audience, the youth. As recommended, using popular television shows like Game of Thrones or musicians such as Eagles of Death Metal, who were personally involved in the November 15, 2015 Paris attack could be useful in promulgating messages of anti-extremism.

These recommendations serve as a base model for moving forward in counterterrorism efforts that may have a positive impact on the ability of international governments and civilians to truly combat extremism in digital spaces, which does manifest in the physical sphere. The threat of online extremism does not simply encourage recruits to journey to the battlegrounds in Iraq and Syria, but more effectively radicalizes the recruit for reprisals against the government in the name of their chosen ideology or terror organization in their homeland. This threat is exacerbated once the looming diaspora of fighters begins and threatens the tenuous security of nations around the world, but particularly in the West.

As the United States, France, Belgium, and many other nations have witnessed in the last ten months, the risk of lone wolf and small cell terrorism is ever-present (last witnessed in the 2-day bombing event in New York and New Jersey by Ahmad Rahami in mid-September 2016). This means that the potential for recruits who are pre-engaged in extremist content and looking for an avenue to participation in jihad is present, even in the United States. Thus it behooves both the state and civilians alike to be aware of the content consumed online, the signs of radicalization as put forth by trusted experts in political psychology and terrorism studies, and develop the necessary relationships among international actors (leaders, bureaucracy, counterterrorism entities of the state), hacktivists, technological corporations (i.e.: Twitter, Facebook, YouTube), and citizens to combat, counter, and idealistically, eliminate much extremist content from online spaces.

Future research opportunities in the examining and idealistically preventing extremist content online that leads to violent mobilization in physical spaces will remain abundant. Brooking and Singer (2016) argue that in terms of the co-option of social media platforms by terror organizations, the Islamic State is just the first to recognize its potential to instantly magnify the affect of one's ideology and content. Once IS has been physically dismantled it will be important for governments, the civil society as well as researchers to remain vigilant in monitoring the continued spread of the group's ideology and propaganda. Not only online but also on the ground in Syria and Iraq, where a generation of children have now been exposed to the group's message during formative years of development, and may seek to continue the mission for a caliphate in the future.

Yet, of course, the opportunities for social media and the internet to provide a continuous breeding ground for extremism requires digital media researchers, political scientists, computer science professionals, and yes, even hacker organizations cooperate in order to identify patterns of use, platform development and co-option tactics, developing more comprehensive and interconnected plans for countering violent narratives online, etc. Every group is going to use social media platforms differently to indoctrinate and mobilize potential supporters to active participation. As the half of world's adult population who does not have access to the internet (Brooking & Singer, 2016) becomes wired, this development will present a multitude of political and social opportunities for citizens on the ground to come together to promote change, as well as the vast potential for theorists to attempt to find commonalities among various organizations' use of the available technologies.

While it is unlikely that the research community will be able to uncover each new group that will latch onto social media to promote its agenda, perhaps similarities in escalation, propagandizing, and certainly the affective response of targeted audiences will glean patterns among the groups that can lead to more effective and pre-emptive response on the part of governments and civil society. Or in the case of democratic protest movements will provide insight that may help in extending movements beyond the regime's patience. Researchers can find a wealth of information in the raw data provided by Twitter and Facebook API, and construct timelines of narratives that lead to real-time mobilization.

There is also much opportunity for political science as a field to assist in diagnosing emergent political movements and pockets of discontent that may swell from a regional to global conflict due to the egalitarian network society offered via social media. Researching and analyzing patterns of internet-enabled terrorism must be an interdisciplinary endeavor, just as combatting and countering jihadist narratives must be a coordinated effort among the civil society and governments as well as among international governments. Future research will need to combine the underlying causes and political context for mobilization of whatever type of group is spreading a violent narrative online, and the field of digital media studies can provide for more analytical insight as to the steps a group takes to successfully promulgate ideology, images, and communication among potential supporters.

As the fight against digital extremism only begins to enter the international community, it behooves governments and civil societies to acknowledge the reality that in order to effectively combat the spread of narratives that are counterproductive to democratic, inclusive, and peaceful principles, there must be disciplined coordination among affected parties, including between international governments working to solve the same problem (i.e.: the Islamic

State). To reiterate the most important point of this text, solving the problem of extremism manifesting in the physical realm, now must encompass the spread of ideology and content in the digital. There is no victory in combatting the Islamic State or any other extremist group in the future without a base level recognition of the group's utilization of the internet and social media to mobilize, recruit, and spread digitally.

REFERENCES

Brooking, E., & Singer, P. W. (2016, Nov.). War goes Viral. *The Atlantic*. Retrieved from http://www.theatlantic.com/magazine/archive/2016/11/war-goes-viral/501125/

Chotiner, I. (2016, June 13). A Lone Wolf Terrorist is Never Quite Alone. *Slate*. Retrieved from http://www.slate.com/articles/news_and_politics/interrogation/2016/06/why_isis_loves_lone_wolf_terrorists.html

Friedman, T. (2005). *The World is Flat: A Brief History of the Twenty-First Century*. New York: Farrar, Straus, and Giroux.

Gartenstein-Ross, D., & Barr, N. (2016, July 26). The Myth of Lone Wolf Terrorism. *Foreign Affairs*. Retrieved from https://www.foreignaffairs.com/articles/western-europe/2016-07-26/myth-lone-wolf-terrorism

Gerstein, J., & Scholtes, J. (2016, Sept. 27). Comey warns of post-ISIL terrorist 'diaspora'. *Politico*. Retrieved from http://www.politico.com/story/2016/09/islamic-state-diaspora-james-comey-228782

Haddadin, F. (2016, Oct. 7). The Semantics of God in the Middle East. *Foreign Policy Association*. Retrieved from http://foreignpolicyblogs.com/2016/10/07/semantics-god-middle-east/

Jadallah, A. (2016, Oct. 21). As ISIS's Caliphate Crumbles, Jihadist Tactics Are Evolving. *Newsweek*. Retrieved from http://www.newsweek.com/2016/10/21/beating-isis-caliphate-terrorism-jihadism-508559.html

Levitt, M. (2016, March 22). Brussels Attacks Raise Questions on Readiness. *The New York Times*. Retrieved from http://www.nytimes.com/2016/03/23/opinion/brussels-attacks-raise-questions-on-readiness.html

Milton, D. (2016, Oct.). *Communication Breakdown: Unraveling the Islamic State's Media Efforts*. Combatting Terrorism Center at West Point. U.S. Military Academy. Retrieved from https://www.ctc.usma.edu/v2/wp-content/uploads/2016/10/ISMedia_Online.pdf

Obama, B. (2014, Sept. 10). *Statement by the President on ISIL (Degrade and Destroy Speech)*. Retrieved from https://www.whitehouse.gov/the-press-office/2014/09/10/statement-president-isil-1

Sommerville, Q. (2016, Oct. 12). Rebels set up internment camp for IS defectors. *BBC News.* Retrieved from http://www.bbc.com/news/world-middle-east-37629679

Szep, J. (2014, Sept. 11). U.S. wins Arab support for Syria/Iraq military campaign. *Reuters.* Retrieved from http://www.reuters.com/article/us-iraq-crisis-kerry-idUSKBN0H50MA20140911

Trofimov, Y. (2016, Sept. 9). What Happens After ISIS Falls? *The Wall Street Journal.* Retrieved from http://www.wsj.com/articles/what-happens-after-isis-falls-1473435007

Related Readings

To continue IGI Global's long-standing tradition of advancing innovation through emerging research, please find below a compiled list of recommended IGI Global book chapters and journal articles in the areas of cyber terrorism, anarchy, and terrorism. These related readings will provide additional information and guidance to further enrich your knowledge and assist you with your own research.

Al Mazari, A., Anjariny, A. H., Habib, S. A., & Nyakwende, E. (2016). Cyber Terrorism Taxonomies: Definition, Targets, Patterns, Risk Factors, and Mitigation Strategies. *International Journal of Cyber Warfare & Terrorism, 6*(1), 1–12. doi:10.4018/IJCWT.2016010101

Al-Saggaf, Y. (2016). Understanding Online Radicalisation Using Data Science. *International Journal of Cyber Warfare & Terrorism, 6*(4), 13–27. doi:10.4018/IJCWT.2016100102

Altheide, D. L. (2014). The Triumph of Fear: Connecting the Dots about Whistleblowers and Surveillance. *International Journal of Cyber Warfare & Terrorism, 4*(1), 1–7. doi:10.4018/ijcwt.2014010101

Arcuri, M. C., Brogi, M., & Gandolfi, G. (2016). Cyber Risk: A Big Challenge in Developed and Emerging Markets. In B. Gupta, D. Agrawal, & S. Yamaguchi (Eds.), *Handbook of Research on Modern Cryptographic Solutions for Computer and Cyber Security* (pp. 80–95). Hershey, PA: IGI Global. doi:10.4018/978-1-5225-0105-3.ch004

Aydin, F., & Pusatli, O. T. (2015). Cyber Attacks and Preliminary Steps in Cyber Security in National Protection. In J. Richet (Ed.), *Cybersecurity Policies and Strategies for Cyberwarfare Prevention* (pp. 269–285). Hershey, PA: IGI Global. doi:10.4018/978-1-4666-8456-0.ch010

Ayish, M. (2014). Employing of Media during Terrorism. In M. Eid (Ed.), *Exchanging Terrorism Oxygen for Media Airwaves: The Age of Terroredia* (pp. 157–170). Hershey, PA: IGI Global. doi:10.4018/978-1-4666-5776-2.ch011

Ayres, N., Maglaras, L., & Janicke, H. (2017). OSNs as Cyberterrorist Weapons against the General Public. In M. Korstanje (Ed.), *Threat Mitigation and Detection of Cyber Warfare and Terrorism Activities* (pp. 179–197). Hershey, PA: IGI Global. doi:10.4018/978-1-5225-1938-6.ch008

Bamrara, A. (2017). Identifying and Analyzing the Latent Cyber Threats in Developing Economies. In M. Moore (Ed.), *Cybersecurity Breaches and Issues Surrounding Online Threat Protection* (pp. 74–94). Hershey, PA: IGI Global. doi:10.4018/978-1-5225-1941-6.ch004

Brown, C. S. (2015). Cyber-Attacks, Retaliation and Risk: Legal and Technical Implications for Nation-States and Private Entities. In J. Richet (Ed.), *Cybersecurity Policies and Strategies for Cyberwarfare Prevention* (pp. 166–203). Hershey, PA: IGI Global. doi:10.4018/978-1-4666-8456-0.ch008

Burmeister, O., Phahlamohlaka, J., & Al-Saggaf, Y. (2015). Good Governance and Virtue in South Africas Cyber Security Policy Implementation. *International Journal of Cyber Warfare & Terrorism*, *5*(1), 19–29. doi:10.4018/IJCWT.2015010102

Čaleta, D. (2016). Cyber Threats to Critical Infrastructure Protection: Public Private Aspects of Resilience. In M. Hadji-Janev & M. Bogdanoski (Eds.), *Handbook of Research on Civil Society and National Security in the Era of Cyber Warfare* (pp. 287–304). Hershey, PA: IGI Global. doi:10.4018/978-1-4666-8793-6.ch014

Cardenas-Haro, J. A., & Dawson, M. (2017). Tails Linux Operating System: The Amnesiac Incognito System in Times of High Surveillance, Its Security Flaws, Limitations, and Strengths in the Fight for Democracy. In M. Dawson, M. Eltayeb, & M. Omar (Eds.), *Security Solutions for Hyperconnectivity and the Internet of Things* (pp. 260–271). Hershey, PA: IGI Global. doi:10.4018/978-1-5225-0741-3.ch010

Carneiro, A. D. (2017). Defending Information Networks in Cyberspace: Some Notes on Security Needs. In M. Dawson, D. Kisku, P. Gupta, J. Sing, & W. Li (Eds.), *Developing Next-Generation Countermeasures for Homeland Security Threat Prevention* (pp. 354–375). Hershey, PA: IGI Global. doi:10.4018/978-1-5225-0703-1.ch016

Chen, J. Q. (2014). A Framework for Cybersecurity Strategy Formation. *International Journal of Cyber Warfare & Terrorism*, *4*(3), 1–10. doi:10.4018/ijcwt.2014070101

Chen, J. Q. (2016). Deception Detection in Cyber Conflicts: A Use Case for the Cybersecurity Strategy Formation Framework. *International Journal of Cyber Warfare & Terrorism*, *6*(3), 31–42. doi:10.4018/IJCWT.2016070103

Cheong, D. D. (2016). Countering Online Violent Extremism: State Action as Strategic Communication. In M. Khader, L. Neo, G. Ong, E. Mingyi, & J. Chin (Eds.), *Combating Violent Extremism and Radicalization in the Digital Era* (pp. 283–306). Hershey, PA: IGI Global. doi:10.4018/978-1-5225-0156-5.ch014

Cheong, P. H. (2014). New Media and Terrorism. In M. Eid (Ed.), *Exchanging Terrorism Oxygen for Media Airwaves: The Age of Terroredia* (pp. 184–196). Hershey, PA: IGI Global. doi:10.4018/978-1-4666-5776-2.ch013

Conway, M. (2014). From "Cyberterrorism" to "Online Radicalism". In M. Eid (Ed.), *Exchanging Terrorism Oxygen for Media Airwaves: The Age of Terroredia* (pp. 198–217). Hershey, PA: IGI Global. doi:10.4018/978-1-4666-5776-2.ch014

Cooley, J. (2014). The Covert Strengthening of Islamic Extremists under Ronald Reagan and George W. Bush. *International Journal of Cyber Warfare & Terrorism*, *4*(4), 17–28. doi:10.4018/ijcwt.2014100102

Crosston, M. D. (2017). The Fight for Cyber Thoreau: Distinguishing Virtual Disobedience from Digital Destruction. In M. Korstanje (Ed.), *Threat Mitigation and Detection of Cyber Warfare and Terrorism Activities* (pp. 198–219). Hershey, PA: IGI Global. doi:10.4018/978-1-5225-1938-6.ch009

Danino, O. (2015). Conflict in Cyberspace: The Case of the Middle East. In J. Richet (Ed.), *Cybersecurity Policies and Strategies for Cyberwarfare Prevention* (pp. 286–306). Hershey, PA: IGI Global. doi:10.4018/978-1-4666-8456-0.ch011

Dawson, M. (2015). A Brief Review of New Threats and Countermeasures in Digital Crime and Cyber Terrorism. In M. Dawson & M. Omar (Eds.), *New Threats and Countermeasures in Digital Crime and Cyber Terrorism* (pp. 1–7). Hershey, PA: IGI Global. doi:10.4018/978-1-4666-8345-7.ch001

Dawson, M. (2017). Exploring Secure Computing for the Internet of Things, Internet of Everything, Web of Things, and Hyperconnectivity. In M. Dawson, M. Eltayeb, & M. Omar (Eds.), *Security Solutions for Hyperconnectivity and the Internet of Things* (pp. 1–12). Hershey, PA: IGI Global. doi:10.4018/978-1-5225-0741-3.ch001

Dawson, M., & Adeboje, W. (2017). Islamic Extremists in Africa: Security Spotlight on Kenya and Nigeria. In M. Dawson, D. Kisku, P. Gupta, J. Sing, & W. Li (Eds.), *Developing Next-Generation Countermeasures for Homeland Security Threat Prevention* (pp. 93–103). Hershey, PA: IGI Global. doi:10.4018/978-1-5225-0703-1.ch005

Dawson, M., Omar, M., & Abramson, J. (2015). Understanding the Methods behind Cyber Terrorism. In M. Khosrow-Pour (Ed.), *Encyclopedia of Information Science and Technology* (3rd ed.; pp. 1539–1549). Hershey, PA: IGI Global. doi:10.4018/978-1-4666-5888-2.ch147

Dawson, M., Omar, M., Abramson, J., Leonard, B., & Bessette, D. (2017). Battlefield Cyberspace: Exploitation of Hyperconnectivity and Internet of Things. In M. Dawson, D. Kisku, P. Gupta, J. Sing, & W. Li (Eds.), *Developing Next-Generation Countermeasures for Homeland Security Threat Prevention* (pp. 204–235). Hershey, PA: IGI Global. doi:10.4018/978-1-5225-0703-1.ch010

de Silva, E., & de Silva, E. (2016). The USA Electrical Grid: Public Perception, Cyber Attacks, and Inclement Weather. In E. de Silva (Ed.), *National Security and Counterintelligence in the Era of Cyber Espionage* (pp. 47–61). Hershey, PA: IGI Global. doi:10.4018/978-1-4666-9661-7.ch003

de Silva, E., de Silva, E., & Nepomuceno, E. B. (2016). Combating Terrorism through Peace Education: Online Educational Perspective. In E. de Silva (Ed.), *National Security and Counterintelligence in the Era of Cyber Espionage* (pp. 203–216). Hershey, PA: IGI Global. doi:10.4018/978-1-4666-9661-7.ch012

Dean, G. (2016). Framing the Challenges of Online Violent Extremism: "Policing-Public-Policies-Politics" Framework. In M. Khader, L. Neo, G. Ong, E. Mingyi, & J. Chin (Eds.), *Combating Violent Extremism and Radicalization in the Digital Era* (pp. 226–259). Hershey, PA: IGI Global. doi:10.4018/978-1-5225-0156-5.ch012

Dillon, L. (2016). Cyberterrorism: Using the Internet as a Weapon of Destruction. In M. Khader, L. Neo, G. Ong, E. Mingyi, & J. Chin (Eds.), *Combating Violent Extremism and Radicalization in the Digital Era* (pp. 426–451). Hershey, PA: IGI Global. doi:10.4018/978-1-5225-0156-5.ch021

Downing, J. (2014). Media Representations of Terrorism. In M. Eid (Ed.), *Exchanging Terrorism Oxygen for Media Airwaves: The Age of Terroredia* (pp. 61–79). Hershey, PA: IGI Global. doi:10.4018/978-1-4666-5776-2.ch005

Eid, M. (2014). New Terrorism and Media. In M. Eid (Ed.), *Exchanging Terrorism Oxygen for Media Airwaves: The Age of Terroredia* (pp. 172–183). Hershey, PA: IGI Global. doi:10.4018/978-1-4666-5776-2.ch012

Eid, M. (2014). Questioning Media Responsibility during Terrorism. In M. Eid (Ed.), *Exchanging Terrorism Oxygen for Media Airwaves: The Age of Terroredia* (pp. 247–260). Hershey, PA: IGI Global. doi:10.4018/978-1-4666-5776-2.ch017

Eid, M. (2014). Terroredia: Exchanging Terrorism Oxygen for Media Airwaves. In M. Eid (Ed.), *Exchanging Terrorism Oxygen for Media Airwaves: The Age of Terroredia* (pp. 1–12). Hershey, PA: IGI Global. doi:10.4018/978-1-4666-5776-2.ch001

Eid, M. (2014). Understanding Terrorism. In M. Eid (Ed.), *Exchanging Terrorism Oxygen for Media Airwaves: The Age of Terroredia* (pp. 15–32). Hershey, PA: IGI Global. doi:10.4018/978-1-4666-5776-2.ch002

Eid, M. (2016). Ethics, Decision-Making, and Risk Communication in the Era of Terroredia: The Case of ISIL. *International Journal of Technoethics*, *7*(2), 91–104. doi:10.4018/IJT.2016070106

Erçetin, Ş. Ş., & Açıkalın, Ş. N. (2016). Is President Erdoğan Really a Dictator?: The Illusion of the Opposition Parties in Turkey. In Ş. Erçetin & H. Bağcı (Eds.), *Handbook of Research on Chaos and Complexity Theory in the Social Sciences* (pp. 1–18). Hershey, PA: IGI Global. doi:10.4018/978-1-5225-0148-0.ch001

Erikha, F., Putra, I. E., & Sarwono, S. W. (2016). ISIS Discourse in Radical Islamic Online News Media in Indonesia: Supporter or Opponent. In M. Khader, L. Neo, G. Ong, E. Mingyi, & J. Chin (Eds.), *Combating Violent Extremism and Radicalization in the Digital Era* (pp. 70–90). Hershey, PA: IGI Global. doi:10.4018/978-1-5225-0156-5.ch004

Fianyi, I., & Zia, T. (2016). Biometric Technology Solutions to Countering Todays Terrorism. *International Journal of Cyber Warfare & Terrorism*, *6*(4), 28–40. doi:10.4018/IJCWT.2016100103

Fisogni, P. (2014). Lone Wolves: Updating the Concept of Enemy in the Social Media Age. *International Journal of Cyber Warfare & Terrorism*, *4*(1), 36–44. doi:10.4018/ijcwt.2014010105

Galliott, J. (2016). Cyber Warfare, Asymmetry, and Responsibility: Considerations for Defence Theorem. In M. Hadji-Janev & M. Bogdanoski (Eds.), *Handbook of Research on Civil Society and National Security in the Era of Cyber Warfare* (pp. 1–21). Hershey, PA: IGI Global. doi:10.4018/978-1-4666-8793-6.ch001

Govil, T., & Govil, J. (2015). Health Information Technology/BioDefense Needs to Fight Bio-Terrorism. In M. Khosrow-Pour (Ed.), *Encyclopedia of Information Science and Technology* (3rd ed.; pp. 3366–3375). Hershey, PA: IGI Global. doi:10.4018/978-1-4666-5888-2.ch330

Grobler, M., Jacobs, P., & van Niekerk, B. (2017). Cyber Security Centres for Threat Detection and Mitigation. In M. Korstanje (Ed.), *Threat Mitigation and Detection of Cyber Warfare and Terrorism Activities* (pp. 21–51). Hershey, PA: IGI Global. doi:10.4018/978-1-5225-1938-6.ch002

Hackett, R. (2014). Understanding Media during Times of Terrorism. In M. Eid (Ed.), *Exchanging Terrorism Oxygen for Media Airwaves: The Age of Terroredia* (pp. 33–43). Hershey, PA: IGI Global. doi:10.4018/978-1-4666-5776-2.ch003

Hadji-Janev, M. (2016). Changing the Approach to Deterrence in Cyberspace while Protecting Civilians from Cyber Conflict. In M. Hadji-Janev & M. Bogdanoski (Eds.), *Handbook of Research on Civil Society and National Security in the Era of Cyber Warfare* (pp. 261–286). Hershey, PA: IGI Global. doi:10.4018/978-1-4666-8793-6.ch013

Hansen, L. L. (2016). Baby Steps: Urban Violence, Gangs, and School Safety. In S. Harding & M. Palasinski (Eds.), *Global Perspectives on Youth Gang Behavior, Violence, and Weapons Use* (pp. 19–35). Hershey, PA: IGI Global. doi:10.4018/978-1-4666-9938-0.ch002

Harding, S. (2016). From "Little Flowers of the Motherland" into "Carnivorous Plants": The Changing Face of Youth Gang Crime in Contemporary China. In S. Harding & M. Palasinski (Eds.), *Global Perspectives on Youth Gang Behavior, Violence, and Weapons Use* (pp. 295–325). Hershey, PA: IGI Global. doi:10.4018/978-1-4666-9938-0.ch014

Heickerö, R. (2016). Cyber Espionage and Illegitimate Information Retrieval. *International Journal of Cyber Warfare & Terrorism*, *6*(1), 13–23. doi:10.4018/IJCWT.2016010102

Heusel, J. (2016). Postracial Justice and the Trope of the "Race Riot". In S. Gibson & A. Lando (Eds.), *Impact of Communication and the Media on Ethnic Conflict* (pp. 195–212). Hershey, PA: IGI Global. doi:10.4018/978-1-4666-9728-7.ch012

Hirshfield, L., Bobko, P., Barelka, A. J., Costa, M. R., Funke, G. J., Mancuso, V. F., & Knott, B. A. et al. (2015). The Role of Human Operators Suspicion in the Detection of Cyber Attacks. *International Journal of Cyber Warfare & Terrorism*, *5*(3), 28–44. doi:10.4018/IJCWT.2015070103

Ho, S. M., & Hollister, J. M. (2015). Cyber Insider Threat in Virtual Organizations. In M. Khosrow-Pour (Ed.), *Encyclopedia of Information Science and Technology* (3rd ed.; pp. 1517–1525). Hershey, PA: IGI Global. doi:10.4018/978-1-4666-5888-2.ch145

Hu, W. (2016). Psychological Effects of the Threat of ISIS: A Preliminary Inquiry of Singapore Case Studies. In M. Khader, L. Neo, G. Ong, E. Mingyi, & J. Chin (Eds.), *Combating Violent Extremism and Radicalization in the Digital Era* (pp. 168–173). Hershey, PA: IGI Global. doi:10.4018/978-1-5225-0156-5.ch009

Huhtinen, A. (2015). The Double Edge of the Information Sword. *International Journal of Cyber Warfare & Terrorism*, *5*(2), 21–30. doi:10.4018/IJCWT.2015040102

Huhtinen, A., Hirvelä, A., & Kangasmaa, T. (2014). The Opportunities of National Cyber Strategy and Social Media in the Rhizome Networks. *International Journal of Cyber Warfare & Terrorism*, *4*(2), 23–34. doi:10.4018/ijcwt.2014040102

Hui, J. Y. (2016). Social Media Analytics for Intelligence and Countering Violent Extremism. In M. Khader, L. Neo, G. Ong, E. Mingyi, & J. Chin (Eds.), *Combating Violent Extremism and Radicalization in the Digital Era* (pp. 328–348). Hershey, PA: IGI Global. doi:10.4018/978-1-5225-0156-5.ch016

Hurley, J. S., McGibbon, H. M., & Everetts, R. (2014). Cyber Readiness: Are We There Yet? *International Journal of Cyber Warfare & Terrorism*, *4*(3), 11–26. doi:10.4018/ijcwt.2014070102

Injac, O., & Šendelj, R. (2016). National Security Policy and Strategy and Cyber Security Risks. In M. Hadji-Janev & M. Bogdanoski (Eds.), *Handbook of Research on Civil Society and National Security in the Era of Cyber Warfare* (pp. 22–48). Hershey, PA: IGI Global. doi:10.4018/978-1-4666-8793-6.ch002

Ismail, S., Sitnikova, E., & Slay, J. (2016). SCADA Systems Cyber Security for Critical Infrastructures: Case Studies in Multiple Sectors. *International Journal of Cyber Warfare & Terrorism*, *6*(3), 79–95. doi:10.4018/IJCWT.2016070107

Jacobsen, J. T. (2014). Clausewitz and the Utility of Cyberattacks in War. *International Journal of Cyber Warfare & Terrorism*, *4*(4), 1–16. doi:10.4018/ijcwt.2014100101

Jaitner, M. (2014). Countering Threats: A Comprehensive Model for Utilization of Social Media for Security and Law Enforcement Authorities. *International Journal of Cyber Warfare & Terrorism*, *4*(2), 35–45. doi:10.4018/ijcwt.2014040103

Janbek, D. (2014). Functioning of Terrorism. In M. Eid (Ed.), *Exchanging Terrorism Oxygen for Media Airwaves: The Age of Terroredia* (pp. 144–156). Hershey, PA: IGI Global. doi:10.4018/978-1-4666-5776-2.ch010

Johansson, F., Kaati, L., & Sahlgren, M. (2016). Detecting Linguistic Markers of Violent Extremism in Online Environments. In M. Khader, L. Neo, G. Ong, E. Mingyi, & J. Chin (Eds.), *Combating Violent Extremism and Radicalization in the Digital Era* (pp. 374–390). Hershey, PA: IGI Global. doi:10.4018/978-1-5225-0156-5.ch018

Johnson, R. (2016). Forensic Psychological Perspectives on Youth Gang Involvement in Juvenile Fire Setting and Bomb Making Weapons Cases: Forensic Perspective Youth Gangs Fire Setting and Weapons. In S. Harding & M. Palasinski (Eds.), *Global Perspectives on Youth Gang Behavior, Violence, and Weapons Use* (pp. 80–100). Hershey, PA: IGI Global. doi:10.4018/978-1-4666-9938-0.ch005

Jones, D. M. (2016). Surveillance and Resistance: Online Radicalization and the Political Response. In E. de Silva (Ed.), *National Security and Counterintelligence in the Era of Cyber Espionage* (pp. 122–143). Hershey, PA: IGI Global. doi:10.4018/978-1-4666-9661-7.ch007

Jones, N., Baines, P., Craig, R., Tunnicliffe, I., & O'Shaughnessy, N. (2015). The Islamist Cyberpropaganda Threat and Its Counter-Terrorism Policy Implications. In J. Richet (Ed.), *Cybersecurity Policies and Strategies for Cyberwarfare Prevention* (pp. 341–366). Hershey, PA: IGI Global. doi:10.4018/978-1-4666-8456-0.ch013

Keating, P. (2016). Games for Social Change: Review of the Potential for Multi Player Online Gaming to Facilitate the Emergence and Growth of Progressive Movements for Social Change within Youth and Community Work. *International Journal of Game-Based Learning*, *6*(4), 73–86. doi:10.4018/IJGBL.2016100105

Keenan, S. J., & Rush, J. P. (2016). A Brief History of School Violence and Disturbance in America. In G. Crews (Ed.), *Critical Examinations of School Violence and Disturbance in K-12 Education* (pp. 1–12). Hershey, PA: IGI Global. doi:10.4018/978-1-4666-9935-9.ch001

Khader, M. (2016). What We Know and What Else We Need to Do to Address the Problem of Violent Extremism Online: Concluding Chapter. In M. Khader, L. Neo, G. Ong, E. Mingyi, & J. Chin (Eds.), *Combating Violent Extremism and Radicalization in the Digital Era* (pp. 486–495). Hershey, PA: IGI Global. doi:10.4018/978-1-5225-0156-5.ch024

Köroğlu, C. Z., & Köroğlu, M. A. (2016). Two Faces of the Reality: New Social Movements. *International Journal of Art, Culture and Design Technologies*, *5*(1), 13–34. doi:10.4018/IJACDT.2016010102

Korstanje, M. E. (2015). Conflictive Touring: The Roots of Terrorism. *International Journal of Cyber Warfare & Terrorism*, *5*(2), 53–67. doi:10.4018/IJCWT.2015040104

Korstanje, M. E. (2015). Terrorists Tend to Target Innocent Tourists: A Radical Review. *International Journal of Cyber Warfare & Terrorism*, *5*(3), 45–54. doi:10.4018/IJCWT.2015070104

Korstanje, M. E. (2017). English Speaking Countries and the Culture of Fear: Understanding Technology and Terrorism. In M. Korstanje (Ed.), *Threat Mitigation and Detection of Cyber Warfare and Terrorism Activities* (pp. 92–110). Hershey, PA: IGI Global. doi:10.4018/978-1-5225-1938-6.ch005

Korstanje, M. E. (2017). Introduction to Tourism Security: Tourism in the Age of Terrorism. In P. Vasant, & K. M. (Eds.), Handbook of Research on Holistic Optimization Techniques in the Hospitality, Tourism, and Travel Industry (pp. 208-226). Hershey, PA: IGI Global. doi: 10.4018/978-1-5225-1054-3.ch009

Korstanje, M. E. (2017). The Risk, the Real, and the Impossibility of Life: Examining the Matrix. In M. Korstanje (Ed.), *Threat Mitigation and Detection of Cyber Warfare and Terrorism Activities* (pp. 163–177). Hershey, PA: IGI Global. doi:10.4018/978-1-5225-1938-6.ch007

Korstanje, M. E. (2017). The Roots of Terror: The Lesser Evil Doctrine under Criticism. In M. Korstanje (Ed.), *Threat Mitigation and Detection of Cyber Warfare and Terrorism Activities* (pp. 254–270). Hershey, PA: IGI Global. doi:10.4018/978-1-5225-1938-6.ch011

Kostyuchenko, Y. V., & Yuschenko, M. (2017). Methods and Tools of Big Data Analysis for Terroristic Behavior Study and Threat Identification: Illegal Armed Groups during the Conflict in Donbas Region (East Ukraine) in Period 2014-2015. In M. Korstanje (Ed.), *Threat Mitigation and Detection of Cyber Warfare and Terrorism Activities* (pp. 52–66). Hershey, PA: IGI Global. doi:10.4018/978-1-5225-1938-6.ch003

Kovacevic, A., & Nikolic, D. (2015). Cyber Attacks on Critical Infrastructure: Review and Challenges. In M. Cruz-Cunha & I. Portela (Eds.), *Handbook of Research on Digital Crime, Cyberspace Security, and Information Assurance* (pp. 1–18). Hershey, PA: IGI Global. doi:10.4018/978-1-4666-6324-4.ch001

Krotofil, M. (2014). Cyber Can Kill and Destroy Too: Blurring Borders Between Conventional and Cyber Warfare. *International Journal of Cyber Warfare & Terrorism*, *4*(3), 27–42. doi:10.4018/ijcwt.2014070103

Lauger, T. R. (2016). The Reality and Myth of Weapons and Violence in Gang Life. In S. Harding & M. Palasinski (Eds.), *Global Perspectives on Youth Gang Behavior, Violence, and Weapons Use* (pp. 60–79). Hershey, PA: IGI Global. doi:10.4018/978-1-4666-9938-0.ch004

Leccisotti, F. Z., Chiesa, R., & De Nicolo, D. (2016). Analysis of Possible Future Global Scenarios in the Field of Cyber Warfare: National Cyber Defense and Cyber Attack Capabilities. In M. Hadji-Janev & M. Bogdanoski (Eds.), *Handbook of Research on Civil Society and National Security in the Era of Cyber Warfare* (pp. 181–204). Hershey, PA: IGI Global. doi:10.4018/978-1-4666-8793-6.ch009

Leccisotti, F. Z., Chiesa, R., De Scalzi, N., Gudas, L., & De Nicolo, D. (2016). Attack Scenarios Perpetrated by Terrorist Organizations Through the Use of IT and ICT: On the Basis of What Is Already Available Today. In M. Hadji-Janev & M. Bogdanoski (Eds.), *Handbook of Research on Civil Society and National Security in the Era of Cyber Warfare* (pp. 102–126). Hershey, PA: IGI Global. doi:10.4018/978-1-4666-8793-6.ch005

Leenen, L., & Meyer, T. (2016). Semantic Technologies and Big Data Analytics for Cyber Defence. *International Journal of Cyber Warfare & Terrorism*, *6*(3), 53–64. doi:10.4018/IJCWT.2016070105

Leurs, K. (2016). Young Connected Migrants and Non-Normative European Family Life: Exploring Affective Human Right Claims of Young E-Diasporas. *International Journal of E-Politics*, *7*(3), 15–34. doi:10.4018/IJEP.2016070102

Liaropoulos, A. N. (2016). Reconceptualising Cyber Security: Safeguarding Human Rights in the Era of Cyber Surveillance. *International Journal of Cyber Warfare & Terrorism*, *6*(2), 32–40. doi:10.4018/IJCWT.2016040103

Linden, J. (2015). Listening to the City: Eleven Years Later—Rebuilding the World Trade Center—New York City—ODR Helps Determine the 9/11 World Trade Center Memorial. In S. Edwards III & D. Santos (Eds.), *Revolutionizing the Interaction between State and Citizens through Digital Communications* (pp. 176–199). Hershey, PA: IGI Global. doi:10.4018/978-1-4666-6292-6.ch010

Lukin, K. (2016). Russian Cyberwarfare Taxonomy and Cybersecurity Contradictions between Russia and EU: An Analysis of Management, Strategies, Standards, and Legal Aspects. In M. Hadji-Janev & M. Bogdanoski (Eds.), *Handbook of Research on Civil Society and National Security in the Era of Cyber Warfare* (pp. 144–161). Hershey, PA: IGI Global. doi:10.4018/978-1-4666-8793-6.ch007

Maitra, D. R. (2016). "It's a Vicious Game": Youth Gangs, Street Violence, and Organised Crime in Modern Britain. In S. Harding & M. Palasinski (Eds.), *Global Perspectives on Youth Gang Behavior, Violence, and Weapons Use* (pp. 192–214). Hershey, PA: IGI Global. doi:10.4018/978-1-4666-9938-0.ch010

Maitra, D. R. (2016). An Exploratory Study of Prison Gangs in Contemporary Society. In S. Harding & M. Palasinski (Eds.), *Global Perspectives on Youth Gang Behavior, Violence, and Weapons Use* (pp. 215–237). Hershey, PA: IGI Global. doi:10.4018/978-1-4666-9938-0.ch011

Marlin, R. (2014). Media-Related Strategies and "War on Terrorism". In M. Eid (Ed.), *Exchanging Terrorism Oxygen for Media Airwaves: The Age of Terroredia* (pp. 124–142). Hershey, PA: IGI Global. doi:10.4018/978-1-4666-5776-2.ch009

Martin, G. (2017). Types of Terrorism. In M. Dawson, D. Kisku, P. Gupta, J. Sing, & W. Li (Eds.), *Developing Next-Generation Countermeasures for Homeland Security Threat Prevention* (pp. 1–16). Hershey, PA: IGI Global. doi:10.4018/978-1-5225-0703-1.ch001

Martin, S. M. (2017). Transnational Crime and the American Policing System. In M. Dawson, D. Kisku, P. Gupta, J. Sing, & W. Li (Eds.), *Developing Next-Generation Countermeasures for Homeland Security Threat Prevention* (pp. 72–92). Hershey, PA: IGI Global. doi:10.4018/978-1-5225-0703-1.ch004

Mastors, E., & Campos, J. H. (2016). Intelligence Studies, Theory, and Intergroup Conflict and Resolution: Theory and Beyond. In E. de Silva (Ed.), *National Security and Counterintelligence in the Era of Cyber Espionage* (pp. 247–258). Hershey, PA: IGI Global. doi:10.4018/978-1-4666-9661-7.ch014

Maximiliano, K. (2017). Risk, Terrorism, and Tourism Consumption: The End of Tourism. In P. Vasant, & K. M. (Eds.), Handbook of Research on Holistic Optimization Techniques in the Hospitality, Tourism, and Travel Industry (pp. 263-285). Hershey, PA: IGI Global. doi: 10.4018/978-1-5225-1054-3.ch012

Mezher, T., El Khatib, S., & Sooriyaarachchi, T. M. (2015). Cyberattacks on Critical Infrastructure and Potential Sustainable Development Impacts. *International Journal of Cyber Warfare & Terrorism*, *5*(3), 1–18. doi:10.4018/IJCWT.2015070101

Musa, W. (2015). Cybercrimes Technologies and Approaches. In M. Cruz-Cunha & I. Portela (Eds.), *Handbook of Research on Digital Crime, Cyberspace Security, and Information Assurance* (pp. 193–210). Hershey, PA: IGI Global. doi:10.4018/978-1-4666-6324-4.ch013

Nacos, B. L. (2014). Tactics of Terrorism. In M. Eid (Ed.), *Exchanging Terrorism Oxygen for Media Airwaves: The Age of Terroredia* (pp. 110–123). Hershey, PA: IGI Global. doi:10.4018/978-1-4666-5776-2.ch008

Neo, L. S. (2016). An Internet-Mediated Pathway for Online Radicalisation: RECRO. In M. Khader, L. Neo, G. Ong, E. Mingyi, & J. Chin (Eds.), *Combating Violent Extremism and Radicalization in the Digital Era* (pp. 197–224). Hershey, PA: IGI Global. doi:10.4018/978-1-5225-0156-5.ch011

Neo, L. S., Dillon, L., Shi, P., Tan, J., Wang, Y., & Gomes, D. (2016). Understanding the Psychology of Persuasive Violent Extremist Online Platforms. In M. Khader, L. Neo, G. Ong, E. Mingyi, & J. Chin (Eds.), *Combating Violent Extremism and Radicalization in the Digital Era* (pp. 1–15). Hershey, PA: IGI Global. doi:10.4018/978-1-5225-0156-5.ch001

Neo, L. S., Shi, P., Dillon, L., Tan, J., Wang, Y., & Gomes, D. (2016). Why Is ISIS so Psychologically Attractive? In M. Khader, L. Neo, G. Ong, E. Mingyi, & J. Chin (Eds.), *Combating Violent Extremism and Radicalization in the Digital Era* (pp. 149–167). Hershey, PA: IGI Global. doi:10.4018/978-1-5225-0156-5.ch008

Nobles, C. (2017). Cyber Threats in Civil Aviation. In M. Dawson, M. Eltayeb, & M. Omar (Eds.), *Security Solutions for Hyperconnectivity and the Internet of Things* (pp. 272–301). Hershey, PA: IGI Global. doi:10.4018/978-1-5225-0741-3.ch011

Nowotny, K. M., Zhao, Q., Kaplan, C., Cepeda, A., & Valdez, A. (2016). Gender Dynamics of Violent Acts among Gang Affiliated Young Adult Mexican American Men. In S. Harding & M. Palasinski (Eds.), *Global Perspectives on Youth Gang Behavior, Violence, and Weapons Use* (pp. 159–173). Hershey, PA: IGI Global. doi:10.4018/978-1-4666-9938-0.ch008

Palma, O. (2016). Criminal Interests within Political Insurgencies: The Case for Development-Centred Counterinsurgency. In F. Cante & H. Quehl (Eds.), *Handbook of Research on Transitional Justice and Peace Building in Turbulent Regions* (pp. 421–443). Hershey, PA: IGI Global. doi:10.4018/978-1-4666-9675-4.ch021

Pang, J. S. (2016). Understanding Personality and Person-Specific Predictors of Cyber-Based Insider Threat. In M. Khader, L. Neo, G. Ong, E. Mingyi, & J. Chin (Eds.), *Combating Violent Extremism and Radicalization in the Digital Era* (pp. 107–128). Hershey, PA: IGI Global. doi:10.4018/978-1-5225-0156-5.ch006

Pant, M. (2017). A Region of Association and Turbulence. In S. Bute (Ed.), *Intercultural Relations and Ethnic Conflict in Asia* (pp. 1–27). Hershey, PA: IGI Global. doi:10.4018/978-1-5225-0582-2.ch001

Poposka, V. (2016). Right to Life and Cyber Warfare: Applicability of Legal Regimes during Counterterrorist Operations (International Humanitarian Law). In M. Hadji-Janev & M. Bogdanoski (Eds.), *Handbook of Research on Civil Society and National Security in the Era of Cyber Warfare* (pp. 450–474). Hershey, PA: IGI Global. doi:10.4018/978-1-4666-8793-6.ch020

Pressman, D. E., & Ivan, C. (2016). Internet Use and Violent Extremism: A Cyber-VERA Risk Assessment Protocol. In M. Khader, L. Neo, G. Ong, E. Mingyi, & J. Chin (Eds.), *Combating Violent Extremism and Radicalization in the Digital Era* (pp. 391–409). Hershey, PA: IGI Global. doi:10.4018/978-1-5225-0156-5.ch019

Pretorius, B., & van Niekerk, B. (2016). Cyber-Security for ICS/SCADA: A South African Perspective. *International Journal of Cyber Warfare & Terrorism*, *6*(3), 1–16. doi:10.4018/IJCWT.2016070101

Ramakrishna, K. (2016). Towards a Comprehensive Approach to Combating Violent Extremist Ideology in the Digital Space: The Counter-Ideological Response (CIR) Model. In M. Khader, L. Neo, G. Ong, E. Mingyi, & J. Chin (Eds.), *Combating Violent Extremism and Radicalization in the Digital Era* (pp. 260–282). Hershey, PA: IGI Global. doi:10.4018/978-1-5225-0156-5.ch013

Ramluckan, T., Ally, S. E., & van Niekerk, B. (2017). Twitter Use in Student Protests: The Case of South Africa's #FeesMustFall Campaign. In M. Korstanje (Ed.), *Threat Mitigation and Detection of Cyber Warfare and Terrorism Activities* (pp. 220–253). Hershey, PA: IGI Global. doi:10.4018/978-1-5225-1938-6.ch010

Rizza, C., Pereira, Â. G., & Curvelo, P. (2014). Do-it-Yourself Justice: Considerations of Social Media use in a Crisis Situation: The Case of the 2011 Vancouver Riots. *International Journal of Information Systems for Crisis Response and Management*, *6*(4), 42–59. doi:10.4018/IJISCRAM.2014100104

Rohn, E., White, C. M., & Leshem, G. (2016). Offensive Information Warfare Revisited: Social Media Use in Man-Made Crises. *International Journal of Information Systems and Social Change*, *7*(2), 1–26. doi:10.4018/IJISSC.2016040101

Romyn, D., & Kebbell, M. (2016). Using the Internet to Plan for Terrorist Attack. In M. Khader, L. Neo, G. Ong, E. Mingyi, & J. Chin (Eds.), *Combating Violent Extremism and Radicalization in the Digital Era* (pp. 91–105). Hershey, PA: IGI Global. doi:10.4018/978-1-5225-0156-5.ch005

S., S., & R., P. (2017). Cybercrime Investigation. In M. Moore (Ed.), *Cybersecurity Breaches and Issues Surrounding Online Threat Protection* (pp. 96-120). Hershey, PA: IGI Global. doi:10.4018/978-1-5225-1941-6.ch005

Saifudeen, O. A. (2016). Getting out of the Armchair: Potential Tipping Points for Online Radicalisation. In M. Khader, L. Neo, G. Ong, E. Mingyi, & J. Chin (Eds.), *Combating Violent Extremism and Radicalization in the Digital Era* (pp. 129–148). Hershey, PA: IGI Global. doi:10.4018/978-1-5225-0156-5.ch007

Saltman, E. M. (2016). Western Female Migrants to ISIS: Propaganda, Radicalisation, and Recruitment. In M. Khader, L. Neo, G. Ong, E. Mingyi, & J. Chin (Eds.), *Combating Violent Extremism and Radicalization in the Digital Era* (pp. 174–196). Hershey, PA: IGI Global. doi:10.4018/978-1-5225-0156-5.ch010

Sereno, K. (2014). Identifying Hyperlink Strategies as a Tool to Discover the Connections between Offline and Online Politics. In A. Solo (Ed.), *Handbook of Research on Political Activism in the Information Age* (pp. 60–80). Hershey, PA: IGI Global. doi:10.4018/978-1-4666-6066-3.ch004

Shahpari, H., & Hojjat, T. A. (2016). Middle East Studies and Muslim Experience after September 11th, 2001: Rebellion against Islamic Ideology and the New Counter-Jihadis. In *Islamic Economy and Social Mobility: Cultural and Religious Considerations* (pp. 272–291). Hershey, PA: IGI Global. doi:10.4018/978-1-4666-9731-7.ch011

Shi, P. (2016). A Supplementary Intervention to Deradicalisation: CBT-Based Online Forum. In M. Khader, L. Neo, G. Ong, E. Mingyi, & J. Chin (Eds.), *Combating Violent Extremism and Radicalization in the Digital Era* (pp. 410–424). Hershey, PA: IGI Global. doi:10.4018/978-1-5225-0156-5.ch020

Shin, Y. (2015). The Effects of Terrorism on Tourism and the Media's Role. In S. Kumar, M. Dhiman, & A. Dahiya (Eds.), *International Tourism and Hospitality in the Digital Age* (pp. 141–155). Hershey, PA: IGI Global. doi:10.4018/978-1-4666-8268-9.ch009

Shorer-Zeltser, M., & Ben-Israel, G. M. (2016). Analysis of Success of Mobilization to Terror using Tools of Neuro-Linguistic Programming (NLP). In M. Hadji-Janev & M. Bogdanoski (Eds.), *Handbook of Research on Civil Society and National Security in the Era of Cyber Warfare* (pp. 127–143). Hershey, PA: IGI Global. doi:10.4018/978-1-4666-8793-6.ch006

Shorer-Zeltser, M., & Ben-Israel, G. M. (2016). Developing Discourse and Tools for Alternative Content to Prevent Terror. In E. de Silva (Ed.), *National Security and Counterintelligence in the Era of Cyber Espionage* (pp. 144–160). Hershey, PA: IGI Global. doi:10.4018/978-1-4666-9661-7.ch008

Shortland, N. D. (2016). "On the Internet, Nobody Knows You're a Dog": The Online Risk Assessment of Violent Extremists. In M. Khader, L. Neo, G. Ong, E. Mingyi, & J. Chin (Eds.), *Combating Violent Extremism and Radicalization in the Digital Era* (pp. 349–373). Hershey, PA: IGI Global. doi:10.4018/978-1-5225-0156-5.ch017

Skoll, G. R. (2014). Stealing Consciousness: Using Cybernetics for Controlling Populations. *International Journal of Cyber Warfare & Terrorism*, *4*(1), 27–35. doi:10.4018/ijcwt.2014010104

Stairs, G. A. (2016). The Amplification of the Sunni-Shia Divide through Contemporary Communications Technology: Fear and Loathing in the Modern Middle East. In S. Gibson & A. Lando (Eds.), *Impact of Communication and the Media on Ethnic Conflict* (pp. 214–231). Hershey, PA: IGI Global. doi:10.4018/978-1-4666-9728-7.ch013

Steinfatt, T., & Janbek, D. (2016). Persuasion and Propaganda in War and Terrorism. In M. Khader, L. Neo, G. Ong, E. Mingyi, & J. Chin (Eds.), *Combating Violent Extremism and Radicalization in the Digital Era* (pp. 16–38). Hershey, PA: IGI Global. doi:10.4018/978-1-5225-0156-5.ch002

Tan, J., Wang, Y., & Gomes, D. (2016). Building National Resilience in the Digital Era of Violent Extremism: Systems and People. In M. Khader, L. Neo, G. Ong, E. Mingyi, & J. Chin (Eds.), *Combating Violent Extremism and Radicalization in the Digital Era* (pp. 307–327). Hershey, PA: IGI Global. doi:10.4018/978-1-5225-0156-5.ch015

Tarlow, P. (2016). Tourism, Terrorism, Morality, and Marketing: A Study of the Role of Reciprocity in Tourism Marketing. In A. Nedelea, M. Korstanje, & B. George (Eds.), *Strategic Tools and Methods for Promoting Hospitality and Tourism Services* (pp. 233–246). Hershey, PA: IGI Global. doi:10.4018/978-1-4666-9761-4.ch014

Terzis, G. (2014). Media Stereotypes of Terrorism. In M. Eid (Ed.), *Exchanging Terrorism Oxygen for Media Airwaves: The Age of Terroredia* (pp. 96–108). Hershey, PA: IGI Global. doi:10.4018/978-1-4666-5776-2.ch007

Torok, R. (2016). Social Media and the Use of Discursive Markers of Online Extremism and Recruitment. In M. Khader, L. Neo, G. Ong, E. Mingyi, & J. Chin (Eds.), *Combating Violent Extremism and Radicalization in the Digital Era* (pp. 39–69). Hershey, PA: IGI Global. doi:10.4018/978-1-5225-0156-5.ch003

Valeri, R. M., & Borgeson, K. (2016). Sticks and Stones: When the Words of Hatred become Weapons – A Social Psychological Perspective. In S. Harding & M. Palasinski (Eds.), *Global Perspectives on Youth Gang Behavior, Violence, and Weapons Use* (pp. 101–132). Hershey, PA: IGI Global. doi:10.4018/978-1-4666-9938-0.ch006

Valter, S. (2016). Military vs. Citizens in the Arab Zone: An Assessment from Political Philosophy. In F. Cante & H. Quehl (Eds.), *Handbook of Research on Transitional Justice and Peace Building in Turbulent Regions* (pp. 140–157). Hershey, PA: IGI Global. doi:10.4018/978-1-4666-9675-4.ch007

Van Gilder, B. J., & Massey, Z. B. (2016). Islamaphobic Discourse and Interethnic Conflict: The Influence of News Media Coverage of the ISIS Beheadings on Identity Processes and Intergroup Attitudes. In S. Gibson & A. Lando (Eds.), *Impact of Communication and the Media on Ethnic Conflict* (pp. 147–161). Hershey, PA: IGI Global. doi:10.4018/978-1-4666-9728-7.ch009

van Heerden, R., Chan, P., Leenen, L., & Theron, J. (2016). Using an Ontology for Network Attack Planning. *International Journal of Cyber Warfare & Terrorism*, *6*(3), 65–78. doi:10.4018/IJCWT.2016070106

van Niekerk, B. (2017). Analysis of Cyber-Attacks against the Transportation Sector. In M. Korstanje (Ed.), *Threat Mitigation and Detection of Cyber Warfare and Terrorism Activities* (pp. 68–91). Hershey, PA: IGI Global. doi:10.4018/978-1-5225-1938-6.ch004

Vaseashta, A., Vaseashta, S. B., & Braman, E. W. (2016). Mitigating Unconventional Cyber-Warfare: Scenario of Cyber 9/11. In M. Hadji-Janev & M. Bogdanoski (Eds.), *Handbook of Research on Civil Society and National Security in the Era of Cyber Warfare* (pp. 238–260). Hershey, PA: IGI Global. doi:10.4018/978-1-4666-8793-6.ch012

Vatikiotis, P. (2016). Social Media Activism: A Contested Field. In T. Deželan & I. Vobič (Eds.), *R)evolutionizing Political Communication through Social Media* (pp. 40–54). Hershey, PA: IGI Global. doi:10.4018/978-1-4666-9879-6.ch003

Veerasamy, N., & Grobler, M. (2015). Logic Tester for the Classification of Cyberterrorism Attacks. *International Journal of Cyber Warfare & Terrorism*, *5*(1), 30–46. doi:10.4018/IJCWT.2015010103

Vega, D. O. (2016). Twitter and Blogs in Social Movements: Ayotzinapa around the World. In A. Fox (Ed.), *Global Perspectives on Media Events in Contemporary Society* (pp. 28–40). Hershey, PA: IGI Global. doi:10.4018/978-1-4666-9967-0.ch003

Virkar, S. (2014). The Changing Face of Electronic Aggression: The Phenomenon of Online Trolling within the Context of e-Participation in the United Kingdom. *International Journal of Cyber Warfare & Terrorism*, *4*(4), 29–46. doi:10.4018/ijcwt.2014100103

Virkar, S. (2016). The Mirror Has Two Faces: Terrorist Use of the Internet and the Challenges of Governing Cyberspace. In E. de Silva (Ed.), *National Security and Counterintelligence in the Era of Cyber Espionage* (pp. 1–27). Hershey, PA: IGI Global. doi:10.4018/978-1-4666-9661-7.ch001

Virkar, S. (2017). Trolls Just Want to Have Fun: Electronic Aggression within the Context of E-Participation and Other Online Political Behaviour in the United Kingdom. In M. Korstanje (Ed.), *Threat Mitigation and Detection of Cyber Warfare and Terrorism Activities* (pp. 111–162). Hershey, PA: IGI Global. doi:10.4018/978-1-5225-1938-6.ch006

Vishwanath, A. (2016). Spear Phishing: The Tip of the Spear Used by Cyber Terrorists. In M. Khader, L. Neo, G. Ong, E. Mingyi, & J. Chin (Eds.), *Combating Violent Extremism and Radicalization in the Digital Era* (pp. 469–484). Hershey, PA: IGI Global. doi:10.4018/978-1-5225-0156-5.ch023

Wang, P. (2016). Death by Hacking: The Emerging Threat of Kinetic Cyber. In M. Khader, L. Neo, G. Ong, E. Mingyi, & J. Chin (Eds.), *Combating Violent Extremism and Radicalization in the Digital Era* (pp. 452–468). Hershey, PA: IGI Global. doi:10.4018/978-1-5225-0156-5.ch022

Wang, Q. (2014). Applicability of Jus in Bello in Cyber Space: Dilemmas and Challenges. *International Journal of Cyber Warfare & Terrorism*, *4*(3), 43–62. doi:10.4018/ijcwt.2014070104

West, L. A., Martin, R. V., Perkins, C., Quatel, J. M., & Macgregor-Skinner, G. (2016). Opposing Viewpoints on Youth Social Media Banning in the U.S. for the Combatance of Extremist Recruiting: Constitutionality and Societal Implications. *International Journal of Cyber Warfare & Terrorism*, *6*(4), 1–12. doi:10.4018/IJCWT.2016100101

White, J. R. (2014). Terrorism Manifestations. In M. Eid (Ed.), *Exchanging Terrorism Oxygen for Media Airwaves: The Age of Terroredia* (pp. 45–60). Hershey, PA: IGI Global. doi:10.4018/978-1-4666-5776-2.ch004

White, R. (2016). Youth Gangs and Youth Violence in Australia. In S. Harding & M. Palasinski (Eds.), *Global Perspectives on Youth Gang Behavior, Violence, and Weapons Use* (pp. 327–345). Hershey, PA: IGI Global. doi:10.4018/978-1-4666-9938-0.ch015

Winch, S. P. (2014). From "Angry Arab" to "Arab Spring". In M. Eid (Ed.), *Exchanging Terrorism Oxygen for Media Airwaves: The Age of Terroredia* (pp. 218–229). Hershey, PA: IGI Global. doi:10.4018/978-1-4666-5776-2.ch015

Yang, K. C., & Kang, Y. (2017). Social Media, Political Mobilization, and Citizen Engagement: A Case Study of the March 18, 2014, Sunflower Student Movement in Taiwan. In M. Adria & Y. Mao (Eds.), *Handbook of Research on Citizen Engagement and Public Participation in the Era of New Media* (pp. 360–388). Hershey, PA: IGI Global. doi:10.4018/978-1-5225-1081-9.ch020

Zulaika, J., & Douglass, W. A. (2014). Questioning Terrorism/Counterterrorism Rationality. In M. Eid (Ed.), *Exchanging Terrorism Oxygen for Media Airwaves: The Age of Terroredia* (pp. 231–246). Hershey, PA: IGI Global. doi:10.4018/978-1-4666-5776-2.ch016

Compilation of References

Ackerman, S., Stephen, C., & MacAskill, E. (2016, Aug. 1). US launches airstrikes against ISIS in Libya. *The Guardian.* Retrieved from https://www.theguardian.com/world/2016/aug/01/us-airstrikes-against-isis-libya-pentagon

Adams, Z. (2016). Fighting the Islamic State in the Fifth Domain: Transnational Terrorism in the Indo-Pacific. *SIR Journal of International Relations.* Retrieved from http://www.sirjournal.org/research/fighting-the-islamic-state

Alder, J. (2013, April 16). Meet the First Digital Generation. Now Get Ready to Play by Their Rules. *Wired.* Retrieved from https://www.wired.com/2013/04/genwired/

Amarasingam, A. (2015, Dec. 30). What Twitter Really Means for Islamic State Supporters. *War on the Rocks.* Retrieved from http://warontherocks.com/2015/12/what-twitter-really-means-for-islamic-state-supporters/

Apps, P. (2015, Dec. 29). Major poll says 74% of Britons expect a major terrorist attack in 2016. *The Independent.* Retrieved from http://www.independent.co.uk/news/uk/home-news/2016-predictions-polled-britons-say-donald-trump-will-disappear-from-us-politics-and-uk-will-suffer-a6789686.html

Arquilla, J., & Ronfeldt, D. (1993). *Cyberwar is Coming!* RAND Corporation. Retrieved from http://www.rand.org/pubs/reprints/RP223.html

Arquilla, J., & Ronfeldt, D. (1996). *The Advent of Netwar.* RAND Corporation. Retrieved from http://www.rand.org/pubs/monograph_reports/MR789.html

Arquilla, J., & Ronfeldt, D. (2000). *Swarming and the Future of Conflict.* RAND Corporation. Retrieved from http://www.rand.org/pubs/documented_briefings/DB311.html

Arquilla, J., & Ronfeldt, D. (2001). *Networks and Netwars: The Future of Terror, Crime, and Militancy*. RAND Corporation. Retrieved from http://www.rand.org/pubs/monograph_reports/MR1382.html

Arquilla, J., & Ronfeldt, D., & Zanini, M. (2000, April). Information-Age Terrorism. *Current History (New York, N.Y.)*, *99*(636), 179–185.

Bakker, E., & de Graaf, B. (2011). Preventing Lone Wolf Terrorism: some CT Approaches Addressed. *Perspectives on Terrorism*, *5*(5-6).

BBC. (2011, Jan. 4). Anonymous activists target Tunisian government sites. *BBC News*. Retrieved from http://www.bbc.com/news/technology-12110892

Berger, J. M. (2015, March 6). *The ISIS Twitter census: Making sense of ISIS's use of Twitter*. Brookings Institute. Retrieved from https://www.brookings.edu/blog/order-from-chaos/2015/03/06/the-isis-twitter-census-making-sense-of-isiss-use-of-twitter/

Berger, J. M., & Strathearn, B. (2013). Who Matters Online: Measuring Influence, Evaluating Content and Countering Violent Extremism in Online Social Networks. *Developments in Radicalization and Political Violence*. International Centre for the Study of Radicalization and Political Violence. Retrieved from http://icsr.info/wp-content/uploads/2013/03/ICSR_Berger-and-Strathearn.pdf

Bergin. (2008, April 5). Facebook terrorism investigation. *The Advertiser*.

Bertram, L. (2016). Terrorism, the Internet and the Social Media Advantage: Exploring how terrorist organizations exploit aspects of the internet, social media and how these same platforms could be used to counter-violent extremism. *Journal for Deradicalization*, (7), 225-252.

Bill C-51. (2015). *Canadian Legislation*. Retrieved from https://openparliament.ca/bills/41-2/C-51/

Bjelopera, J. P. (2013). American Jihadist Terrorism: Combating a Complex Threat. *Congressional Research Service*. Retrieved from https://www.fas.org/sgp/crs/terror/R41416.pdf

Bogage, J. (2016, June 14). This hacker is fighting ISIS by spamming its Twitter accounts with porn. *Washington Post*. Retrieved from https://www.washingtonpost.com/news/the-switch/wp/2016/06/14/this-hacker-is-fighting-isis-by-spamming-its-twitter-accounts-with-porn/

Borchers, C. (2015, Nov. 28). How will 'Anonymous' wage war on the Islamic State? One of its own tells us. *The Washington Post.* Retrieved from https://www.washingtonpost.com/news/the-fix/wp/2015/11/28/how-will-anonymous-wage-war-on-the-islamic-state-one-of-its-own-tells-us/

Brachman, J. (2008). *Global Jihadism: Theory and Practice*. New York: Routledge.

Brooking, E., & Singer, P. W. (2016, Nov.). War goes Viral. *The Atlantic.* Retrieved from http://www.theatlantic.com/magazine/archive/2016/11/war-goes-viral/501125/

Brown, P., & Bruer, W. (2015, Feb. 3). *FBI Official: ISIS is recruiting teens.* Retrieved from http://www.cnn.com/2015/02/03/politics/fbi-isis-counterterrorism-michael-steinbach/

Browne, R., & Starr, P. (2016, June 20). CIA director grave warning: ISIS dangerous as ever. *CNN.* Retrieved from http://www.cnn.com/2016/06/16/politics/john-brennan-cia-isis/

Burke, J. (2016, Feb. 25). How the changing media is changing terrorism. *The Guardian.* Retrieved from https://www.theguardian.com/world/2016/feb/25/how-changing-media-changing-terrorism

CAGE. (2016, Sept. 29). *The 'science' of pre-crime: The secret 'radicalisation' study underpinning PREVENT*. Retrieved from http://cage.ngo/publication/the-science-of-pre-crime/

Cammaerts, B. (2007). Citizenship, the Public Sphere, and Media. In Reclaiming the Media: Communication Rights and Democratic Media Roles, (pp. 1-9). Intellect Books, University of Chicago Press.

Chotiner, I. (2016, June 13). A Lone Wolf Terrorist is Never Quite Alone. *Slate.* Retrieved from http://www.slate.com/articles/news_and_politics/interrogation/2016/06/why_isis_loves_lone_wolf_terrorists.html

Chu, H. (2009). Next Generation of Terrorism: Ubiquitous Cyber Terrorism with the Accumulation of all Intangible Fears. *Journal of Universal Computer Science*, *15*(12), 2373–2386.

Clarke, R., & Knake, R. (2010). *Cyber War: The Next Threat to National Security and What to Do About It*. New York: Harper Collins.

Coleman, G. (2011). From the Lulz to Collective Action. *The New Everyday: A Media Commons Project, 6.*

Conway, M. (2006). Terrorism and the Internet: New Media- New Threat? *Parliamentary Affairs*, *59*(2), 283–298. doi:10.1093/pa/gsl009

Cooper, H. (2016, April 20). Boko Haram and ISIS are collaborating more, U.S. military says. *New York Times.* Retrieved from http://www.nytimes.com/2016/04/21/world/africa/boko-haram-and-isis-are-collaborating-more-us-military-says.html

Cornish, P., Livingstone, D., Clemente, D., & Yorke, C. (2010). *On cyber warfare: A Chatham House Report*. The Royal Institute of International Affairs.

Cosgrove, B., & Bhowmick, N. (2013, Aug. 5). Terror at the Olympics: Munich, 1972. *Time.* Retrieved from http://time.com/24489/munich-massacre-1972-olympics-photos/

Couch, N., & Robins, B. (2013). *Big Data for Defence and Security*. Occasional Paper, Royal United Services Institute. Retrieved from https://www.ndm.net/datawarehouse/pdf/big-data-for-defence-and-security-report-final.pdf

Cunningham, E. (2014, Oct. 24). Bomb blast in Egypt's Sinai Peninsula is deadliest attack on army in decades. *Washington Post.* Retrieve from https://www.washingtonpost.com/world/bomb-attack-in-egypts-sinai-peninsula-is-deadliest-attack-on-its-army-in-years/2014/10/24/98d14ad7-91c0-4acd-835f-e61b8f18a434_story.html

Cunningham, K. (2007). Countering Female Terrorism. *Studies in Conflict and Terrorism*, *30*(2), 113–129. doi:10.1080/10576100601101067

Day, J. (2016, March). *The ISIS Bandwagon: Under What Conditions Do Groups Pledge Support?* Boston University Institute on Culture, Religion, and World Affairs. Retrieved from https://www.bu.edu/cura/files/2016/03/The-ISIS-Bandwagon-V3.pdf

Denning, D. (2001). Is Cyber Terror Next? New York: U.S. Social Science Research Council. Retrieved from http://www.ssrc.org/sept11/essays/denning.htm.2001

Denning, D. (2004). Cyberterrorism. In R. A. Spinello & H. V. Tavani (Eds.), *Readings in CyberEthics* (pp. 536–541). Jones and Bartlett.

Dewey, C. (2015, Nov. 23). The secret American origins of Telegram, the encrypted messaging app favored by the Islamic State. *The Washington Post.* Retrieved from https://www.washingtonpost.com/news/the-intersect/wp/2015/11/23/the-secret-american-origins-of-telegram-the-encrypted-messaging-app-favored-by-the-islamic-state/

Dodd, V. (2016, April 14). Counter-terrorism drive for public to report online Isis propaganda. *The Guardian.* Retrieved from https://www.theguardian.com/uk-news/2016/apr/15/police-launch-crackdown-on-isis-internet-extremism

Drennen, J. (2014). Who has Contributed What in the Coalition Against the Islamic State? *Foreign Policy.* Retrieved from http://foreignpolicy.com/2014/11/12/who-has-contributed-what-in-the-coalition-against-the-islamic-state/

Dunham, W., & Beech, E. (2015, March 21). Islamic State calls on backers to kill 100 U.S. military personnel. *Reuters.* Retrieved from http://www.reuters.com/article/us-mideast-crisis-threat-idUSKBN0MH0QQ20150321

Emery, N., Werchan, J., & Mowles, D., Jr. (2005). Fighting Terrorism and Insurgency: Shaping the Information Environment. *Military Review.* Retrieved from http://www.au.af.mil/au/awc/awcgate/milreview/emery.pdf

Fisher, A. (2015). How Jihadist Networks Maintain a Persistent Online Presence. *Perspectives on Terrorism, 9*(3).

Flores, R., & Brennan, M. (2016, Aug. 18). Twitter announces it has suspended 235,000 terror-linked accounts. *CBS News.* Retrieved from http://www.cbsnews.com/news/twitter-announces-it-has-suspended-235000-terror-linked-accounts/

Frenkel, S. (2016, May 12). This is How ISIS uses the Internet. *Buzzfeed News.* Retrieved from https://www.buzzfeed.com/sheerafrenkel/everything-you-ever-wanted-to-know-about-how-isis-uses-the-i?utm_term=.jr0AjwPE5#.vseo9gxq2

Friedman, T. (2005). *The World is Flat: A Brief History of the Twenty-First Century.* New York: Farrar, Straus, and Giroux.

Frontline. (2014). *The Rise of ISIS.* Retrieved from http://www.pbs.org/wgbh/frontline/film/rise-of-isis/

Gartenstein-Ross, D. (2015, Jan. 6). The Decline of ISIS Has Already Begun. *The Atlantic*. Retrieved from http://www.theatlantic.com/international/archive/2015/01/the-decline-of-isis-syria-iraq/384261/

Gartenstein-Ross, D., & Barr, N. (2016, July 26). The Myth of Lone Wolf Terrorism. *Foreign Affairs*. Retrieved from https://www.foreignaffairs.com/articles/western-europe/2016-07-26/myth-lone-wolf-terrorism

Gerstein, J., & Scholtes, J. (2016, Sept. 27). Comey warns of post-ISIL terrorist 'diaspora'. *Politico*. Retrieved from http://www.politico.com/story/2016/09/islamic-state-diaspora-james-comey-228782

Gibbons-Neff, T. (2016, Oct. 11). ISIS used an armed drone to kill two Kurdish fighters and wound French troops, report says. *The Washington Post*. Retrieved from https://www.washingtonpost.com/news/checkpoint/wp/2016/10/11/isis-used-an-armed-drone-to-kill-two-kurdish-fighters-and-wound-french-troops-report-says/

Glavin, N. (2015, Dec. 7). Counter ISIS' Narratives on Social Media. *The New York Times*. Retrieved from http://www.nytimes.com/roomfordebate/2015/12/06/how-can-america-counter-the-appeal-of-isis/counter-isis-narratives-on-social-media

Haddadin, F. (2016, Oct. 7). The Semantics of God in the Middle East. *Foreign Policy Association*. Retrieved from http://foreignpolicyblogs.com/2016/10/07/semantics-god-middle-east/

Hammadi, S., Scammell, R., & Yuhas, A. (2016, July 3). Dhaka cafe attack ends with 20 hostages among dead. *The Guardian*. Retrieved from https://www.theguardian.com/world/2016/jul/01/dhaka-bangladesh-restaurant-attack-hostages

Hanson, F. (2015). *Countering ISIS in Southeast Asia: The case for an ICT offensive*. Perth USAsia Centre. Retrieved from http://perthusasia.edu.au/usac/assets/media/docs/publications/FINAL_F_Hanson_ISIS_ICT.pdf

Hegel, G. W. F., & Miller, A. V. (1977). Force and the Understanding: Appearance and the Supersensible World: Phenomenology of Spirit (5th ed.). New York: Oxford University Press.

Hong, N. (2016, Aug. 28). U.S. Revamps Line of Attack in Social-Media Fight Against Islamic State. *Wall Street Journal*. Retrieved from http://www.wsj.com/articles/u-s-revamps-line-of-attack-in-social-media-fight-against-islamic-state-1472415600

Huey, L., & Witmer, E. (2016). #IS_Fangirl: Exploring a New Role for Women in Terrorism. *Journal of Terrorism Research*, *7*(1), 1–10. doi:10.15664/jtr.1211

Hussain, G., & Saltman, E. (2014). Jihad Trending: A Comprehensive Analysis of Online Extremism and How to Counter It. *Quilliam*. Retrieved from https://www.quilliamfoundation.org/wp/wp-content/uploads/publications/free/jihad-trending-quilliam-report.pdf

Ignatius, D. (2014, Sept. 18). James Clapper: We underestimated the Islamic State's 'will to fight'. *The Washington Post*. Retrieved from https://www.washingtonpost.com/opinions/david-ignatius-we-underestimated-the-islamic-state-james-clapper-says/2014/09/18/f0f17072-3f6f-11e4-9587-5dafd96295f0_story.html?utm_term=.a77014d7cc07

Jadallah, A. (2016, Oct. 21). As ISIS's Caliphate Crumbles, Jihadist Tactics Are Evolving. *Newsweek*. Retrieved from http://www.newsweek.com/2016/10/21/beating-isis-caliphate-terrorism-jihadism-508559.html

Jasparro, C. (2010). *Lone Wolf – The Threat from Independent Jihadists*. Retrieved from https://wikileaks.org/gifiles/attach/168/168290_Osac-jir1209.pdf

Jenkins, B. M. (2006). *The New Age of Terrorism*. RAND Corporation. Retrieved from http://www.rand.org/content/dam/rand/pubs/reprints/2006/RAND_RP1215.pdf

Kam, E. (2015). The Islamic State Surprise: The Intelligence Perspective. *Strategic Assessment*, *18*(3), 21–31.

Karatzogianni, A. (2015, Nov. 18). Anonymous hackers could be Islamic State's online nemesis. *The Conversation*. Retrieved from http://theconversation.com/anonymous-hackers-could-be-islamic-states-online-nemesis-50876

Kholmann, E. (2005, Aug. 2). Al Qaeda and the Internet. *Washington Post*. Retrieved from http://www.washingtonpost.com/wp-dyn/content/discussion/2005/08/05/DI2005080501262.html

Kingsley, P. (2014, June 23). Who is behind ISIS's terrifying online propaganda operation? *The Guardian.* Retrieved from https://www.theguardian.com/world/2014/jun/23/who-behind-isis-propaganda-operation-iraq

Kirk, A. (2016, March 24). Iraq and Syria: How many foreign fighters are fighting for Isil. *The Telegraph.* Retrieved from http://www.telegraph.co.uk/news/2016/03/29/iraq-and-syria-how-many-foreign-fighters-are-fighting-for-isil/

Koehler, D. (2014). The Radical Online: Individual Radicalization Processes and the Role of the Internet. *Journal for Deradicalization.* (1). Retrieved from http://journals.sfu.ca/jd/index.php/jd/article/view/8/8

Koerner, B. (2016, June 12). The Orlando Nightclub Shooting could have been an ISIS plan with ISIS knowing nothing about it. *Wired.* Retrieved from https://www.wired.com/2016/06/orlando-massacre-shows-isis-outsources-terror/

Levitt, M. (2016, March 22). Brussels Attacks Raise Questions on Readiness. *The New York Times.* Retrieved from http://www.nytimes.com/2016/03/23/opinion/brussels-attacks-raise-questions-on-readiness.html

Levs, J., & Yan, H. (2014, Sept. 22). Western allies reject ISIS leader's threats against their civilians. *CNN News.* Retrieved from http://www.cnn.com/2014/09/22/world/meast/isis-threatens-west/

Livingstone, S. (2004). The challenge of changing audiences or, what is the audience researcher to do in the age of the Internet? *European Journal of Communication*, *19*(1), 75–86. doi:10.1177/0267323104040695

Marks, T. A., Gorka, L. S., & Sharp, R. (2010). *Getting the next war right: Beyond population-centric warfare.* Institute for National Strategic Studies.

Masi, A. (2015, May 11). ISIS-Affiliated Hackers Threaten Cyberattacks, 'Electronic War' on US, Europe. *International Business Times.* Retrieved from http://www.ibtimes.com/isis-affiliated-hackers-threaten-cyberattacks-electronic-war-us-europe-1917320

Mastracci, D. (2015, March 2). Islamophobia sells in Canada. *Al Jazeera America.* Retrieved from http://america.aljazeera.com/opinions/2015/3/islamophobia-sells-in-canada.html

Mele, C. (2016, Sept. 27). Pepe the Frog Meme Listed as a Hate Symbol. *The New York Times.* Retrieved from http://www.nytimes.com/2016/09/28/us/pepe-the-frog-is-listed-as-a-hate-symbol-by-the-anti-defamation-league.html

Miller, G., & Higham, S. (2015, May 8). In a propaganda war against ISIS, the U.S. tried to play by the enemy's rules. *Washington Post*. Retrieved from https://www.washingtonpost.com/world/national-security/in-a-propaganda-war-us-tried-to-play-by-the-enemys-rules/2015/05/08/6eb6b732-e52f-11e4-81ea-0649268f729e_story.html

Milton, D. (2016, Oct.). *Communication Breakdown: Unraveling the Islamic State's Media Efforts*. Combatting Terrorism Center at West Point. U.S. Military Academy. Retrieved from https://www.ctc.usma.edu/v2/wp-content/uploads/2016/10/ISMedia_Online.pdf

Nacos, B., Bloch-Elkon, Y., & Shapiro, R. (2007). Post-9/11 Terrorism Threats, News Coverage, and Public Perceptions in the United States. *International Journal of Conflict and Violence*, *1*(2), 105–126.

Naim, M. (2014, June 19). The Rise of Militarized NGOs. *The Atlantic*. Retrieved from http://www.theatlantic.com/international/archive/2014/06/the-rise-of-militarized-ngos/373074/

Navarro, J., & Villaverde, J. (2014). The future of counter-terrorism in Europe. The need to be lost in the correct direction. *European Journal of Future Research*, *2*(50).

Neumann, P. (2012). *Countering Online Radicalization in America*. Bipartisan Policy Center. Retrieved from http://bipartisanpolicy.org/wp-content/uploads/sites/default/files/BPC%20_Online%20Radicalization%20Report.pdf

New America. (n.d.). *Fighting ISIS in the Information Space*. Retrieved from https://www.newamerica.org/international-security/events/fighting-isis-information-space/

New York Times. (2015, November). *Attack in Paris*. Retrieved from http://www.nytimes.com/news-event/attacks-in-paris

Newman, L. (2016, June 8). France releases terror alert app. *Slate*. Retrieved from http://www.slate.com/blogs/future_tense/2016/06/08/france_releases_terror_alert_app.html

Obama, B. (2014, Sept. 10). *Statement by the President on ISIL (Degrade and Destroy Speech)*. Retrieved from https://www.whitehouse.gov/the-press-office/2014/09/10/statement-president-isil-1

Precht, T. (2008). Homegrown Terrorism and Islamist Radicalisation in Europe: From Conversion to Terrorism. An Assessment of the Factors Influencing Violent Islamist Extremism and Suggestions for Counter Radicalisation Measures. Copenhagen: Danish Ministry of Defence. Retrieved from http://www.justitsministeriet.dk/sites/default/files/media/Arbejdsomraader/Forskning/Forskningspuljen/2011/2007/Home_grown_terrorism_and_Islamist_radicalisation_in _Europe_-_an_assessment_of_influencing_factors__2_.pdf

Prucha, N. (2011). Online Territories of Terror – Utilizing the Internet for Jihadist Endeavors. *Orient (Paris)*, iv.

Prucha, N. (2014). Celebrities of the Afterlife: Death Cult, Stars, and Fandom of Jihadist Propaganda. In R. Lohlker & T. Abu Hamdeh (Eds.), *Jihadi Thought and Ideology, Jihadism and Terrorism* (Vol. 1, p. 135). Berlin: Logos.

Reuters. (2016, July 20). *100 jihadis still entering Syria from Turkey each week*. Retrieved from http://www.reuters.com/article/us-mideast-crisis-syria-idUSKCN1000VU

Rogan, H. (2006). *JIHADISM ONLINE - A study of how al-Qaida and radical Islamist groups use the Internet for terrorist purposes*. Transnational Radical Islamism Project. Norwegian Defence Research Establishment. Retrieved from http://www.ffi.no/no/Rapporter/06-00915.pdf

Ross, W. (2016, May 18). Chibok girls: Kidnapped schoolgirl found in Nigeria. *BBC News*. Retrieved from http://www.bbc.com/news/world-africa-36321249

Russon, M. (2016, Jan. 14). Alrawi: ISIS has built secure Android messaging app to replace Telegram, says Anonymous affiliate GhostSec. *International Business Times*. Retrieved from http://www.ibtimes.co.uk/alrawi-isis-builds-secure-android-messaging-app-replace-telegram-says-anonymous-affiliate-ghostsec-1537948

Schatz, B. (2015, Nov. 24). Inside Anonymous' Messy Cyberwar Against ISIS. *Mother Jones*. Retrieved from http://www.motherjones.com/politics/2015/11/anonymous-hacking-isis-ghost-security

Sharma, S. (2015, June 4). Islamic State has an English-language radio broadcast that sounds eerily like NPR. *The Washington Post*. Retrieved from https://www.washingtonpost.com/news/worldviews/wp/2015/06/04/islamic-state-has-a-daily-english-language-radio-broadcast-that-sounds-eerily-like-it-could-be-on-npr/

Shinkman, P. (2016, Sept. 27). Military Success Against ISIS Will Create 'Terrorist Diaspora,' James Comey Says. *U.S. News*. Retrieved from http://www.usnews.com/news/articles/2016-09-27/military-success-against-isis-will-create-terrorist-diaspora-james-comey-says

Sommerville, Q. (2016, Oct. 12). Rebels set up internment camp for IS defectors. *BBC News*. Retrieved from http://www.bbc.com/news/world-middle-east-37629679

Soriano, M. (2008). Terrorism and the Mass Media after Al Qaeda: A Change of Course? *Athena Intelligence Journal*, *3*(1), 1–20.

Spaaij, R. (2010). The Enigma of Lone Wolf Terrorism: An Assessment. *Studies in Conflict and Terrorism*, *33*(9), 854–870. doi:10.1080/1057610X.2010.501426

Starr, B. (2016, Sept. 13). US bombs ISIS chemical weapons plant. *CNN News*. Retrieved from http://www.cnn.com/2016/09/13/politics/isis-chemical-weapons-plant/

Steinbach, M. (2015, June 3). *Terrorism Gone Viral: The Attack in Garland, Texas and Beyond*. Federal Bureau of Investigations. Statement before the House Homeland Security Committee. Retrieved from https://www.fbi.gov/news/testimony/terrorism-gone-viral-the-attack-in-garland-texas-and-beyond

Stern, J. (2003). *Terror in the Name of God: Why Religious Militants Kill*. New York: HarperCollins.

Strategic Implementation Plan for Empowering Local Partners to Prevent Violent Extremism in the United States. (2011, Dec). Executive Office of the President of the United States. Retrieved from https://www.whitehouse.gov/sites/default/files/sip-final.pdf

Szep, J. (2014, Sept. 11). U.S. wins Arab support for Syria/Iraq military campaign. *Reuters*. Retrieved from http://www.reuters.com/article/us-iraq-crisis-kerry-idUSKBN0H50MA20140911

Tadjdeh, Y. (2015, April). *Big Data Helping to Pinpoint Terrorist Activities, Attacks*. Retrieved from http://www.nationaldefensemagazine.org/archive/2015/April/Pages/BigDataHelpingtoPinpointTerroristActivitiesAttacks.aspx

Talbot, D. (2015, Sept. 30). Fighting ISIS Online. *MIT Technology Review*. Retrieved from https://www.technologyreview.com/s/541801/fighting-isis-online/

Teich, S. (2013, Oct.). Trends and Developments in Lone Wolf Terrorism in the Western World. *International Institute for Counter-Terrorism.* Retrieved from http://www.ctcitraining.org/docs/LoneWolf_SarahTeich2013.pdf

The Daily Express. (2016, Dec. 9). *More than half of Germans see refugees as country's biggest problem.* Retrieved from http://www.express.co.uk/news/world/741822/Germany-Merkel-migrant-crisis-refugees-integration-biggest-problem

The Economist. (2016, April 18). *Israel is using social media to prevent terrorist attacks.* Retrieved from http://www.economist.com/news/middle-east-and-africa/21697083-new-paradigm-intelligence-israel-using-social-media-prevent-terrorist

Torok, R. (2013). Developing an explanatory model for the process of online radicalization and terrorism. Perth, Australia: Springer. Retrieved from http://www.security-informatics.com/content/2/1/6

Travis, A. (2016, Aug. 24). MPs say Facebook, Twitter and YouTube 'consciously failing' to tackle extremism. *The Guardian.* Retrieved from https://www.theguardian.com/politics/2016/aug/25/mps-facebook-twitter-youtube-extremism-isis

Trofimov, Y. (2016, Feb. 25). How Tunisia Became a Top Source of ISIS Recruits. *The Wall Street Journal.* Retrieved from http://www.wsj.com/articles/how-tunisia-became-a-top-source-of-isis-recruits-1456396203

Trofimov, Y. (2016, Sept. 9). What Happens After ISIS Falls? *The Wall Street Journal.* Retrieved from http://www.wsj.com/articles/what-happens-after-isis-falls-1473435007

Tufecki, Z. (2016, May 19). The Real Bias Built In at Facebook. *The New York Times.* Retrieved from http://www.nytimes.com/2016/05/19/opinion/the-real-bias-built-in-at-facebook.html

Tuysuz, G., & Almasy, S. (2016, July 6). Istanbul airport explosions: 36 dead, 147 injured, Turkish officials say. *CNN News.* Retrieved from http://www.cnn.com/2016/06/28/europe/turkey-istanbul-airport-attacks/

United Nations Security Council. (2014). Resolution 2178. Retrieved from http://www.un.org/en/sc/ctc/docs/2015/SCR%202178_2014_EN.pdf

Verkaik, R. (2015, July 10). Government deradicalisation plan will brand Muslims with beards as terrorists, say academics. *The Independent.* Retrieved from http://www.independent.co.uk/news/uk/politics/government-deradicalisation-plan-will-brand-muslims-with-beards-as-terrorists-say-academics-10381796.html

Vitale, H. M., & Keagle, J. M. (2014). A time to tweet, as well as a time to kill: ISIS's projection of power in Iraq and Syria. *Defense Horizons,* (77). Retrieved from http://search.proquest.com/docview/1618549256?accountid=8289

We left out nuclear targets, for now. (2003, March 3). *The Guardian.* Retrieved from https://www.theguardian.com/world/2003/mar/04/alqaida.terrorism

Weimann, G. (2014). New Terrorism and New Media. Washington, DC: Commons Lab of the Woodrow Wilson International Center for Scholars. Retrieved from https://www.wilsoncenter.org/sites/default/files/STIP_140501_new_terrorism_F.pdf

Weimann, G. (2004). *Cyberterrorism: How Real Is the Threat? Special Research Report*. Washington, DC: United States Institute of Peace.

Weinstein, A. (2015, March 12). Here's How the US Should Fight ISIS With Social Media. *Wired.* Retrieved from https://www.wired.com/2015/03/heres-us-fight-isis-social-media/

Wieviorka, M. (2004). *The making of Terrorism.* Chicago: The University of Chicago Press.

Wire Staff, C. N. N. (2012, May 23). U.S. senators: Al Qaeda calls for 'electronic jihad'. *CNN.* Retrieved from http://www.cnn.com/2012/05/23/politics/al-qaeda-electronic-jihad/

Woodie, A. (2014, Oct. 14). *How Big Data Analytics Can Help Fight ISIS.* Retrieved from https://www.datanami.com/2014/10/14/big-data-analytics-can-help-fight-isis/

Yadron, D. (2015, Oct. 20). Free Services Make the Internet a Privacy Nightmare, Security Researcher Says. *Wall Street Journal.* Retrieved from http://www.wsj.com/articles/free-services-make-the-internet-a-privacy-nightmare-security-researcher-says-1445370168

Young, A. (2015, Nov. 28). How Anonymous Fights ISIS: It's More about Research Than Hacking. *International Business Times.* Retrieved from http://www.ibtimes.com/how-anonymous-fights-isis-its-more-about-research-hacking-2202869

Yourish, K., Watkins, D., Giratikanon, T., & Lee, J. C. (2016, July 16). How Many People Have Been Killed in ISIS Attacks Around the World. *The New York Times.* Retrieved from http://www.nytimes.com/interactive/2016/03/25/world/map-isis-attacks-around-the-world.html

Youssef, N. (2015, Jan. 29). ISIS and Boko Haram's Unholy Online Alliance. *The Daily Beast.* Retrieved from http://www.thedailybeast.com/articles/2015/01/29/isis-and-boko-haram-s-unholy-online-alliance.html

Zelin, A. (2015). Picture Or It Didn't Happen: A Snapshot of the Islamic State's Official Media Output. *Perspectives on Terrorism, 9*(4). Retrieved from http://www.terrorismanalysts.com/pt/index.php/pot/article/view/445/html

Zetter, K. (2014, Nov. 3). An Unprecedented Look at Stuxnet, the World's First Digital Weapon. *Wired.* Retrieved from https://www.wired.com/2014/11/countdown-to-zero-day-stuxnet/

About the Author

Emily Stacey is a Political Science professor. She successfully completed her dissertation defense in November 2016, and will formally graduate from Swansea University (Wales, UK) in Summer 2017. Emily's dissertation research focuses on the necessity of bureaucratization in contemporary social movements, namely those using digital technologies to mobilize and sustain dissent. She has participated in the Digital Methods Initiative at the University of Amsterdam (2013) and the Oxford Internet Institute's Summer Doctoral Program (2014). Emily has published a book chapter as well as a journal article with IGI before this work. Her future research will focus on the use of digital technologies and social media platforms to influence nationalist movements occurring around the world. You can follow Emily on Twitter: @politikphd.

Index

M

P

R

S

T

U

Y

www.ingramcontent.com/pod-product-compliance
Ingram Content Group UK Ltd.
Pitfield, Milton Keynes, MK11 3LW, UK
UKHW050944290926
15470UKWH00005B/1634

9 781522 521907